HRH Princess Tatiana
Diana Farr Louis

A Taste of GREECE

Recipes, Cuisine & Culture

teNeues

Contents

Περιεχόμενα · Periehomena

Welcome!

Καλώς ήρθατε · Kalos irthate

I believe that food is a reflection of ourselves; what and how we choose to eat speaks to the life we want to live. Moving to Greece with my husband, Prince Nikolaos, added a new chapter to my culinary identity and allowed me to redefine what home tastes like. Most importantly, Greek cuisine—being simple but never simplistic, unpretentious but still seductive, and authentic but always evolving—taught me an invaluable lesson: there is no need to camouflage one's true essence and hide behind unnecessary flavors, either in the kitchen or in life.

A splash of olive oil, a pinch of hand-crushed fresh sea salt, and a squeeze of lemon is all that is needed to bring out the real flavors of every dish and make it unique. The same goes for people—one can be most colorful in one's purity and simplicity, even though once in a while we all need to add a bit of spice.

In Greece, food is an integral part of the local culture and national identity. Daily meals continue to bring extended families around the table, creating social bonds and a sense of belonging. A lack of food, however, does exactly the opposite: it not only deprives people of the very basics but also alienates and excludes those who cannot afford to provide for themselves and their loved ones.

Over the last few years, the Greek nonprofit organization Boroume has aimed to help one person and one family at a time by engaging local communities to make meals available to those in need. When I first met with them, I immediately decided to lend my support to a cause that is very close to my heart.

Coordinating this project ever since has been a heartwarming journey that has allowed me not only to connect with a passionate Greek community but also to bring together people from around the world who share my own love for Greece, its cuisine, and its culture. I hope that this book will warm as many hearts and kitchens as possible and that our common love will continue to grow by sharing.

From the bottom of my heart, I thank all who have helped make this book a reality—everyone's enthusiastic response was beyond my expectations.

Tatiana Blatnik

Foreword

Εισαγωγικό σημείωμα · Eisagogiko simeioma

My association with Boroume, the Greek charity whose motto is "Saving lives by saving food," began in February 2012. Greece's crisis, already in its second year, was making news but the picture was inevitably bleaker than I thought it needed to be. I couldn't bear what was happening to my adopted country—the soaring numbers of unemployed, homeless, and hungry, but they were not the whole story. I resolved to start writing articles for The Huffington Post with a different message that would shift people's focus to the good and positive aspects of our misfortune, about what Greeks were doing to help themselves.

My first piece was about a homeless shelter where a friend had been cooking for 10 years. When he started, virtually all his diners were foreigners; now the majority were Greeks and the numbers were growing by the week. My second was about Boroume, then not even a year old, but already winning recognition for its efforts to divert perfectly good food from the trash bins onto people's plates.

My first interview with Xenia Papastavrou, Boroume's founder, took place in a café in Athens before she and her partners even had an office and she was still holding down a full-time job as a journalist. As she told me, "I was an active volunteer at the Greek Food Bank and was wracking my brain to find a way to solve the problem of food waste. So much food was being thrown away, yet so many people were going hungry, and our crisis was in its second year already. I finally worked out the idea and found the name—which means We Can—on May 3, 2011, my youngest son's birthday."

The idea was ingenious because it has a twofold strategy, reducing waste and helping people. By the time I met her, in January 2012, the idea had taken on a third dimension. Briefly, Xenia and her partners, Alexander Theodorides and Alexia Moatsou, had set up Boroume as a "facilitator" that would create links between the haves and have-nots in the same or nearby neighborhoods. With a simple phone call, tavernas, bakers, greengrocers, party givers, and anyone with extra cooked food or fresh fruit and vegetables that could not be sold or used the next day would be put in touch with local institutions: an old-age home, orphanage, school for the handicapped, or even a family that needed assistance. Once the contact was made, the receivers would collect the food and the association could continue without Boroume. The wonderful side benefit has been the development of an increased sense of community, neighbors helping neighbors.

~~During that first interview, I was instantly attracted to Xenia's clear energy, modesty, and drive to help.~~
A year later I returned to Boroume for a progress report and met the team at their sun-filled office on a back street near Central Market. Their enthusiasm was contagious as they told me of their successes, of how the network had expanded well past Athens to the whole country and that donations were pouring in from Europe and the Americas, from individuals, corporations, and even kindergartens in Zurich that made gifts for children here. The atmosphere was so ebullient that I resolved to drop in whenever my own spirits were flagging.

Meanwhile, even though I had stopped writing for The Huffington Post, *Xenia continued to keep me up to date. We became Facebook friends and real friends, appearing once on Diane Kochilas's TV cooking show, and meeting here and there so she could tell me about plans to set up a vegetable garden in a landed orphanage, an adopt a family program, glean farmers' fields after harvesting, persuade a large supermarket chain to give any cooked or fresh food that could not be sold the next day to neighboring institutions—a major accomplishment—and finally, in May 2015, she told me about the idea for this cookbook.*

No, it would not consist of recipes for leftovers; instead, it would be a compendium of testimonials and favorite recipes contributed by well-known personalities of Greek origin living abroad and passionate philhellenes from a variety of professions, linked solely by their deep affection for Greece. All the profits would go to Boroume's sister organization, Friends of Boroume, in the United States and then back to Athens to provide more meals. A relatively new arrival in the city, Tatiana Blatnik, the wife of Prince Nikolaos of Greece, would coordinate the project and had already secured a publisher, teNeues in Germany, who would handle the book. Would I like to be the editor?

Finally able to help my favorite cause, I was both flattered and thrilled. Working with the inspiring Boroume team and with our partners in Germany has been more fun than work, while (minimally) editing the contributions has been a wonderful experience. Reading them was enough to make me fall in love with Greece all over again.

In fact, our team wanted to call this book For the Love of Greece, *for love is its primary ingredient. And we hope that you who buy this book will feel it too, as you read how the country has touched our contributors and as you cook their recipes, both original and classic. With this purchase you are joining Boroume's crusade against food waste and hunger, and this should make each dish even tastier. You, too, are cooking for Greece.*

As Xenia said as we were going to press, "For me, the added value that Boroume brings is not only the thousands of meals a day that it is saving and donating but most importantly, the way that it is doing it. It has turned the problem of food waste on its head and isn't just a successful initiative that helps with food."

Diana Farr Louis

Letter from Boroume

Επιστολή από το Μπορούμε • Epistoli apo to Boroume

Boroume is the only nonprofit organization in Greece dedicated to reducing food waste and fighting malnutrition at the same time. We achieve this primarily by acquiring food from donors of all kinds and offering it to charitable organizations all over the country.

Breaking the mold of the "classical" food saving model, i.e. a food bank with a warehouse and high logistical costs, Boroume has revolutionized food saving. We are able to "rescue" any kind of food, almost anywhere, and direct it to those in need at a fraction of the cost of the traditional model. We achieve this by eliminating logistics; in other words, by linking a food donor with the charitable organization nearest them and coordinating the donation pick-up by the organization itself. This system makes food saving and offering both easy and comprehensive.

We began small, starting in late 2011 with a donation of 12 cheese pies from a bakery in central Athens to a nearby soup kitchen. By February 2016, we had managed to save and offer more than six million food portions from several thousand different donors to more than 600 local charitable organizations all over Greece. By 2016 the ratio of operational cost to saved and offered food portions had risen to 1 €/22 portions; in other words, for every euro donated to Boroume, 22 food portions are transformed from food waste to valuable nutritional support for those in need. This ratio covers not only the running of our food-saving network but also all the additional Boroume programs, which we have created as part of our holistic approach to the issue of food waste and nutritional support.

These programs include those aimed at changing public attitudes towards food waste, such as our "Stop Food Waste" awareness program, "Boroume at School," and "Boroume in the Neighborhood," as well as those involving saving food in the entire food chain, such as "Boroume Gleaning" and "Boroume at the Farmers' Market." There's also our "We Are Family" program, through which we transform monetary donations at 100 percent of their value from all over the world into supermarket vouchers for families facing the harshest food insecurity today in Greece.

Today, Boroume saves and offers more than 15,000 food portions every day, from individuals to the largest food companies, from the farmer to the supermarket and the farmers' market, from a small neighborhood café to the largest café and bakery chains, from all sorts of corporate and social events, restaurants, schools, hotels, hospitals, army camps, even other charitable organizations which have received large food donations which they cannot fully absorb.

All this is driven by our passion to help people in need and is being achieved through collaborations with partners, supporters, and friends, for Boroume does nothing on its own. Ninety percent of our team are volunteers, all our food-saving and offering endeavors are based on working closely with donors and recipient charitable organizations, and our budget is covered by private donations from foundations, individuals, and companies.

The book you have in your hands is the perfect example of these attributes of Boroume's DNA. It is the product of a collaboration of many different people who, driven by their passion to help people in need in Greece, worked together to bring this project to life.

The initial suggestion was made back in the summer of 2012 by Gina Lionatos, a Greek-Australian friend who had just read about Boroume and wished to support our cause. The idea was never rejected, but due to more immediate priorities was left on the shelf for the time being.

In the winter of 2015, during our first meeting with Tatiana Blatnik, who had heard of our organization and wished to support us, we knew instantly that we had found the perfect project manager for this idea. We immediately started discussing the project and very soon teNeues was on board as our publisher. We did not have to ponder long about our editor because Diana Farr Louis, who had supported us from the very beginning with her articles, was the obvious choice for us. Our beloved volunteer and founder of "Friends of Boroume" in the United States, Nick Politakis, was also the obvious choice for coordinator from Boroume.

The same passion was the essential factor in convincing so many distinguished contributors to believe in our cause and support us through their recipes and stories.

It is difficult to express in words the gratitude we feel at Boroume for all the support we have received from all these friends over the past few years and especially during this project. We believe that the best way to say "thank you" is to continue working every day as passionately as ever to alleviate the suffering of many people in Greece by providing them with much-needed food that others have donated, in the easiest and most efficient way possible.

Alexander Theodoridis
Managing Director

ANDREW & RACHEL DALBY

Andrew Dalby writes about the history of food, especially Greek food.
Siren Feasts *(1996) was his first book. He translated the* Byzantine Geoponika *into English (2010). He also wrote* Eleftherios Venizelos *(2010), a biography focusing on Venizelos's work at the Paris Peace Conference. He lives in France and visits Greece as often as he can. He has one major fault: he doesn't cook.*
Rachel Dalby, Andrew's daughter, grew up in England and now lives in Parikia on the island of Paros where she and her partner run the Marina Café and a supermarket. She has no faults. These are three of her recipes. Rachel and Andrew are currently working on a new history of Greek food, with recipes, for Reaktion Books.

WHAT IS YOUR FAVORITE GREEK FOOD?

That's easy. It's fish, fresh, simply prepared, eaten beside the sea. What fish? It'll depend on what there is. Having said fish, I'll stretch the definition to include an octopus once caught and cooked and served by the owner of a restaurant called Porphyra on Paros.
It tasted more real than any other octopus ever has . . . but no use hoping for another like it. The owner has retired now and gone home to Epirus.

IN A FEW WORDS, WHAT DOES GREECE MEAN TO YOU?

The people, the country, the scents of the hillsides, the sea and sky, the scattered islands, each one with its own character. The food of course. But people mostly.

WHAT IS YOUR FONDEST MEMORY OF GREECE?

A walk on Spetses. A dinner in Agios Nikolaos on Crete. A long, fierce political discussion at Brettos Distillery in Athens. A talk about Pontos (Poseidon's predecessor) at the sports center bar in Thessaloniki. A visit to Pyrgi in the Mastihohoria on Chios. Ouzo beside the harbor in Naxos town. Absolute peace in Lefkes on Paros. How could I possibly choose?

Lenten Tahini Cake

Ταχινόπιτα · Tahinopita

This recipe is from the Ragoussis Bakery on Paros. With no eggs, oil, or butter, this is one of the most popular cakes made during Eastern Orthodox Lent, from Clean Monday until Big Friday . . . although moustalevria *(grape must pudding) and* ladopita *(semolina pie) are pretty good, too. This cake has a soft, dense, moist texture. Be sure to stir the tahini well before measuring it, in case the oil has separated.*

1 Preheat the oven to 325°F/170°C. Line the base of an 8-inch/20-cm square cake pan with parchment paper and grease the pan.

2 In a large bowl mix the water, tahini, and sugar together with a stiff whisk or metal spoon. Sift in the flour and baking powder and mix until combined.

3 Pour the mixture into the prepared cake pan, smoothing down the top. Sprinkle sesame seeds over the surface and bake until a skewer inserted in the center comes out clean, 45 to 50 minutes. If the cake starts to brown too quickly, cover it loosely with foil. Let the cake cool in the pan before cutting it into squares and serving.

Ingredients

* ⅔ cup/170 ml water
* ½ cup/150 g tahini
* 1 cup/200 g packed brown sugar
* 1¾ cups/250 g all-purpose flour
* ½ tsp baking powder
* ¼ tsp ground cloves
* Sesame seeds

Cabbage Rice

Λαχανόρυζο · Lahanorizo

*This makes enough for two Greek peasants, or perhaps four if served with a thick slice of feta on the side and some smoked or salted preserved pork (*siglino pasto*) or ham.*

1 Heat the oil in a large pan over medium-low heat, add the onion and carrots, and cook, stirring, until the onion is translucent, at least 10 minutes. Add the cabbage and stir until the vegetables glisten and the cabbage has collapsed in volume, another 5 minutes or so. Add the water, bring to a boil, then reduce the heat and add the rice. Season with salt and pepper to taste, cover, and simmer for 20 minutes. The rice should be soft all the way through, the cabbage and onion should be meltingly tender, and the consistency loose but not too soupy—like a wet risotto.

2 Remove from the heat and set aside, covered, for 10 minutes, then spoon the mixture onto a serving dish, squeeze the lemon juice over it, and serve.

i *To vary this dish, you could add a spoonful or two of homemade or store-bought tomato paste to the cabbage, as it might be served in the Peloponnese; or a very Macedonian handful of soft, stoned prunes stirred in with the rice; or ½ tsp hot paprika with the seasonings for a Thracian or Ionian flavor.*

Ingredients *(Serves 2 to 4)*

* 5 tbsp/75 ml extra-virgin olive oil
* 1 onion, chopped
* 2 carrots, peeled and cut into ¾-in/2-cm chunks
* ½ small green cabbage, cored, cut into 4 pieces, and coarsely chopped
* 2 cups/500 ml water
* 1 cup/200 g arborio rice
* Salt and freshly ground black pepper
* Juice of ½ lemon, plus extra to taste

Beef Stew

Μοσχάρι κοκκινιστό · Moschari kokkinisto

Kokkinisto *is the generic name for the method of cooking a dish in a red wine and tomato sauce. Any meat can be used, as well as snails or frog legs or a variety of vegetables and pulses. One of the most famous versions in the Peloponnese,* kokora kokkinisto, *is made with rooster and eaten with* hilopites *(homemade egg noodles).*
Kokkinisto *is one of the two main types of Greek stews, the second being* lemonato *(with lemon), in which lemon juice and plenty of olive oil replace the tomatoes, and the flavorings include a leafy herb, often dill. This dish cannot be hurried: the meat needs time to harden and then slowly cook to melting softness, so be prepared for a two- or three-hour simmer. As with so many other dishes,* kokkinisto *would rarely be eaten hot from the stove, so you can start well ahead of time. Serve with fried potatoes, spaghetti, or rice, or perhaps with a shredded lettuce salad.*

1 Heat the oil in a large pot or Dutch oven over medium-high heat, add the meat, and brown lightly all over. Add the onion and garlic and pour in a little more oil if the pot is dry. Cook until the onion is softened but not browned. Add the tomato puree, wine, tomato paste, and enough water to mostly cover the meat (just the tops should show, like icebergs). Add the cinnamon, sugar, bay leaf, cloves, and pepper flakes and season with salt and pepper to taste.

2 Cover the pot and simmer until the meat is tender, 2 to 3 hours, stirring occasionally and adding more water if the pot is drying out. Taste the sauce and add more ground cinnamon if desired. (The taste should be pronounced and recognizable but not overpowering.) Serve.

Ingredients *(Serves 4)*

* 2 tbsp olive oil, plus extra if needed
* 1 lb/500 g chuck steak, blade steak, or other stewing steak, trimmed and cut into 1- to 1½-in/3- to 4-cm chunks
* 1 large onion, diced
* 2 garlic cloves, thinly sliced
* 1 (14.5-oz/425-ml) can tomato puree
* 10 tbsp/150 ml strong-flavored dry red wine
* 1 tsp tomato paste
* 1 tsp ground cinnamon (or 1 stick, broken in half), plus extra to taste
* ½ tsp sugar
* 1 bay leaf
* 2 whole cloves
* Pinch red pepper flakes or 1 dried chile, crumbled
* Salt and freshly ground black pepper

HM QUEEN ANNE-MARIE

Queen Anne-Marie, former Queen of the Hellenes, was born in Copenhagen in 1946 at Amalienborg Palace. She is the youngest daughter of King Frederik IX and Queen Ingrid of Denmark. She attended schools in Denmark and Switzerland and is fluent in Greek, English, French, and Danish. Princess Anne-Marie met the then Crown Prince Constantine of Greece in Copenhagen in 1959. In March 1964, King Paul I died after a short illness and his son, Constantine, succeeded him to the Greek throne; King Constantine married Princess Anne-Marie later that year. The couple has five children. As Queen of Greece, Anne-Marie devoted much of her time in Greece to many charities, including helping people in rural areas of Greece and supporting crafts such as embroidery and weaving. Having lived away from Greece for many years they have finally returned and settled by the sea in Porto Heli.

WHAT IS YOUR FAVORITE GREEK FOOD?

The tastes of Greece are unique. Every time I have a tomato in Greece I am amazed by how special it tastes. I also love *kritharaki* (orzo) served hot as *yiouvetsi* (see pp. 122–125) or even cold in the summer as a salad with lots of fresh dill and vegetables. I love the simple Greek yogurt, Greek wild flower honey, and all the herbs—one can drink the scents of Greek hills in a cup of *tsai tou vounou* (mountain tea). The vegetables in Greece are fresh and genuine—grilled or in a salad, you just do not get them anywhere else. Another of my favorite tastes of Greece is the *horiatiki salata* (Greek salad, see p. 30), which we have transformed into a delicious refreshing cold summer soup with the same consistency as gazpacho.

IN A FEW WORDS, WHAT DOES GREECE MEAN TO YOU?

Everything. Greece is a very magical place. From the distinct light to its people, their courage, and their love of their country. Greece has a magnetism that always brings people back, and those who are away sometimes ache with nostalgia and a strong desire to return.

WHAT IS YOUR FONDEST MEMORY OF GREECE?

My wedding, of course. But there are so many other memories . . . A more recent one was when my husband and I celebrated our 50th wedding anniversary back in Athens. It was a very emotional day for me as I was able to have all my children and their respective wives and husbands together. It closed a circle. We had a small blessing in the Athens Cathedral—the same as where we got married. It is a memory that shall stay with me forever, just like our wedding.

Greek Salad Gazpacho

Κρύα σούπα χωριάτικης σαλάτας · *Krya soupa horiatikis salatas*

Ingredients *(Serves 4)*

* 1.7 lb/800 g ripe tomatoes, peeled, seeded, and chopped
* 1 large cucumber, washed, peeled, and chopped
* 1 green bell pepper, seeded and chopped
* 1 white onion, chopped and soaked in ice water for 30 minutes
* 6 tbsp/90 ml olive oil, plus extra for drizzling
* 1–2 tbsp cider vinegar
* ½ tsp dried oregano
* Fresh basil leaves
* Salt and freshly ground white pepper
* 2 oz/55 g feta cheese, crumbled (½ cup)
* 2 tbsp chopped pitted black olives
* 1 barley rusk, crushed, or crisp toast or croutons

1 Put the tomatoes, cucumber, pepper, onion, oil, and vinegar in a food processor or blender and pulse until finely chopped. Add the oregano, a few basil leaves, and salt and pepper to taste. Pulse until you have a puree—you can make it as chunky or as smooth as you like. If you'd like a clear soup, like a consommé, for true elegance, pass the mixture through a fine-mesh strainer. In any case, refrigerate the soup for at least 1 hour before serving.

2 Ladle the soup into bowls, garnish with the feta and olives, drizzle a few drops of oil over the soup and sprinkle with some torn basil leaves. Serve with a dish of crushed barley rusk on the side.

Paximadia, or rusks, are pieces of twice-baked bread that are very popular in Greece. The technique of baking loaves, cutting them into slices, and returning them to the oven until they lose all their moisture goes back to antiquity. It was a way of both preserving bread and conserving precious fuel. Nowadays, though they're no longer a necessity, bakeries and supermarkets are full of them, in different sizes and flavors. Barley rusks may be the favorite, as they are particularly tasty in salads, soaking up the dressing and adding crunch. If you cannot find rusks, use croutons or make your own rusks by cutting slices of any kind of hearty bread and baking them for about 20 minutes in a very low oven. You may find you prefer them to crackers or toast and will always want to have some on hand.

Fish a la Spetsiota

Ψάρι αλά Σπετσιώτα · *Psari ala spetsiota*

Although the name of this dish implies that it originated on the island of Spetses, you'll find it all over Greece. For this recipe you can use a whole fish (a bass or grouper, let's say) or fish fillets. This fish goes well with potatoes or rice.

1. Preheat the oven to 350°F/180°C.

2. Lightly salt the cleaned fish or fillets and let stand for about 30 minutes. Mix the tomatoes, parsley, wine, oil, and garlic in a bowl and let stand for 30 minutes.

3. Season the fish with pepper and pour about one-third of the tomato mixture into a 9 by 13-inch/23 by 33-cm baking pan. Place the fish or fillets on top and cover them with the rest of the tomato mixture. Sprinkle with the breadcrumbs and drizzle a little oil over them. Bake for 20 to 25 minutes until the fish is cooked and the breadcrumbs have formed a crisp, golden crust.

Ingredients *(Serves 4)*

* 4 fish fillets or 1 whole fish, cleaned and gutted (about 2½ lb/1 kg total)
* Sea salt and freshly ground black pepper
* 1½ cups/270 g chopped tomatoes
* 1 bunch chopped fresh parsley
* ½ cup/120 ml dry white wine
* ¼ cup/60 ml olive oil
* 4 chopped garlic cloves
* 1 cup/45 g fresh breadcrumbs
* Extra-virgin olive oil for drizzling

ARIANNA HUFFINGTON

Arianna Huffington is the cofounder, president, and editor-in-chief of The Huffington Post Media Group, *and the author of 15 books. In May 2005, she launched* The Huffington Post, *a news and blog site that quickly became one of the most widely read and frequently cited media brands on the Internet. In 2012, the site won a Pulitzer Prize for national reporting.*

Arianna has been named to Time *magazine's list of the world's 100 most influential people and the Forbes 100 Most Powerful Women list. Originally from Greece, she moved to England when she was 16 and graduated from Cambridge University with an M.A. in economics. At 21, she became president of the famed debating society the Cambridge Union. She serves on numerous boards, including The Center for Public Integrity and The Committee to Protect Journalists.*

Her book, Thrive: The Third Metric to Redefining Success and Creating a Life of Well-Being, Wisdom, and Wonder, *debuted at number one on the* New York Times *Best Seller list. Her newest book,* The Sleep Revolution: Transforming Your Life One Night at a Time, *is about the science, history, and mystery of sleep.*

WHAT IS YOUR FAVORITE GREEK FOOD?
Everything associated with the Christmas and New Year holidays.

IN A FEW WORDS, WHAT DOES GREECE MEAN TO YOU?
Greece, to me, is inseparable from the concept of *filotimo*. Growing up in Athens, *filotimo* was a word I heard all the time. Roughly translated, it means rising above trivialities and living not just for yourself, but for something larger than yourself. And Greece's steep challenges have illuminated a national trait, resilience. I've witnessed that Greek resilience firsthand many times in my life, and it has been awe-inspiring.

WHAT IS YOUR FONDEST MEMORY OF GREECE?
My mother was always cooking, as she believed that if you didn't eat something every 20 minutes, something terrible would happen to you. Growing up in Athens, I looked forward each year to the holidays, when she would bake *melomakárona*, the traditional Greek Christmas cookies. One of my fondest memories is the smell of cloves, honey, cinnamon, orange, and brandy wafting from the kitchen.

Melomakárona (Christmas Cookies)

Μελομακάρονα

Over the Christmas holidays, you won't find a single home in Greece without these scrumptious brown cookies, piled on a platter next to another filled with sugar-dusted kourambiedes, *or almond-shortbread cookies. But they are good at any time of year.*

1 Preheat the oven to 325°F/160°C.

2 Combine the oil, brandy, orange zest and juice, and sugar in a large bowl and beat well. Sift the flour with the baking powder, soda, cinnamon, and cloves into a second bowl. Gradually add the flour to the liquid mixture and knead well for 5 to 6 minutes. Break off small pieces of dough and form small rounds or oval shapes about 3 inches/7 cm long. Place them on an ungreased baking sheet or two if necessary. Once you've finished, gently press each *melomakárona* against the surface of a grater in order to leave a decorative pattern on each one and return it to the sheet. Bake the *melomakárona* until golden, about 30 minutes. Remove them from the oven and let cool on the baking sheet.

3 *For the honey syrup:* Combine the honey, sugar, and water in a medium saucepan and bring to a boil. Skim the foam off the top, add the cinnamon stick, reduce the heat, and simmer until the syrup is thick, 10 minutes. Arrange the cold *melomakárona* on a platter and pour the hot syrup over them. Sprinkle with the crushed walnuts and a little powdered cinnamon.

Ingredients *(Makes about 40 cookies)*

* 2 cups/480 ml olive oil
* 1 cup/240 ml brandy
* Grated zest of 1 orange plus 1 cup/240 ml orange juice
* 1 cup plus 2 tbsp/225 g sugar
* 7 cups/1 kg all-purpose flour, or 5¼ cups/750 g all-purpose flour and 1¾ cups/250 g semolina flour
* 2 tbsp baking powder
* 1 tsp cinnamon, plus extra for sprinkling
* ½ tsp cloves
* 1 tbsp baking soda
* 1 cup/125 g crushed walnuts

Honey Syrup:

* 2 cups/400 g honey
* 2 cups/400 g sugar
* 2 cups/480 ml water
* 1 cinnamon stick

BOB COSTAS

Bob Costas has won 26 Emmy awards, more than any sports broadcaster. His versatility has been recognized with awards in the categories of hosting, play-by-play, writing, journalism, news, and entertainment. He is the only person ever to have won Emmys in news, sports, and entertainment. One of the most recognizable voices in the world of sports, Costas has been a fixture at NBC Sports since 1980 and has covered every major sport over the past three decades. He has been a prominent part of NBC's presentations of 11 Olympics, seven Super Bowls, seven World Series, and 10 NBA Finals, as well as other major events, such as the Kentucky Derby, Preakness, and Belmont, and the U.S. Open Golf Championship. A devoted baseball fan, Bob has been able to return to his first love, baseball, contributing interviews, commentaries, and play-by-play to MLB Network. Beyond his onscreen presence, Costas is a New York Times *Best Selling author and has hosted a number of syndicated radio programs. He was named Sportscaster of the Year by the National Sportswriters and Sportscasters Association for a record eight times, and in June 2012 Costas was inducted into the NSSA Hall of Fame.*

WHAT IS YOUR FAVORITE GREEK FOOD?
Stuffed grape leaves with egg-lemon sauce, Greece in a mouthful.

IN A FEW WORDS, WHAT DOES GREECE MEAN TO YOU?
Greece is the homeland of my grandparents, a cultural influence for many of my relatives, the land of some of the world's greatest historical sites, the birthplace of Democracy . . . and of course, the Olympics.

WHAT IS YOUR FONDEST MEMORY OF GREECE?
That's easy. Hosting the 2004 Athens Olympics and being able to help present not just the drama of the competition, but some of the history of the Olympics, and Greece itself, to millions of American viewers.

Stuffed Grape Leaves

Ντολμάδες · Dolmades

Everybody loves dolmades, and there are almost as many versions as there are cooks. The name comes from the Turkish verb that means "to stuff," and you will also find dolmades made from cabbage, chard, and lettuce leaves, as well as zucchini flowers, though grape leaves are the only ones that Greek cooks freeze or dry for use in the off-season. Grape leaves that have been preserved in brine are available at Greek and Middle Eastern groceries, or in the international aisle of large supermarkets.

Ingredients *(Serves 6 to 8)*

* 1 (14- to 16-oz/400- to 455-g) jar grape leaves in brine or 50 fresh grape leaves
* ¼ cup/60 ml olive oil
* 1 lb/500 g ground sirloin or ground turkey
* 2 eggs, beaten
* 1 onion, chopped
* ½ cup/100 g long-grain rice
* ¼ cup/15 g chopped fresh parsley
* 1 tbsp chopped fresh mint
* Salt and freshly ground black pepper
* 4 cups/960 ml chicken broth

Egg-Lemon Sauce

* 3 eggs
* Juice of 3 lemons

1 Bring a large pot of water to a boil. Rinse the grape leaves well under running water and then boil them for about 3 minutes. Drain in a colander and spread out on paper or dish towels to dry. Remove any hard stems. (Fresh grape leaves need no rinsing but should be similarly parboiled and drained.)

2 Heat the oil in a large skillet over medium heat, add the meat, and cook, stirring, until it loses all traces of pink. Transfer the meat to a large bowl and let cool slightly, then add the eggs, onion, rice, parsley, mint, and salt and pepper to taste. Stir until thoroughly combined.

3 Arrange any torn grape leaves in the bottom of a large pot or Dutch oven. Place several leaves on the counter, shiny side down, with the stem end closest to you. Put a teaspoon of the filling near the base of each leaf, fold the 2 sides over it, and then roll it toward the tip, to make a small cylindrical packet. Place seam-side down in the pot, and repeat with the remaining filling and leaves, layering them in the pot as you go. Don't worry about making them perfect. They won't fall apart if you pack them close together.

4 Pour the broth over the stuffed leaves and place an old plate on top of them (this keeps them from moving). Bring the liquid to a boil, then cover, reduce the heat, and cook for 45 minutes to 1 hour.

5 *For the egg-lemon sauce:* When the dolmades are cooked, beat the eggs in a medium-sized bowl and and beat in the lemon juice. Slowly add some hot broth from the pan, a ladleful at a time, beating constantly. The sauce should be fluffy and foamy. Return it to the pan with the dolmades and shake—don't stir—to distribute it. Serve.

i *For a vegetarian version, omit the meat, increase the rice to 1 cup, and use vegetable broth in place of the chicken broth.*

CAROLE BAMFORD

Carole Bamford is the founder of the British farmshop chain Daylesford Organic as well as her own lines of clothing and bath and body products. Her passion for organic farming, natural clothing, and well-considered beauty products has made her an influential champion of craftsmanship, traditional skills, and natural living. Carole is recognized as a visionary in organic farming and healthy food retailing. She is an energetic promoter of natural products and believes that artisanal skills are to be cherished alongside contemporary design, beauty, and function.
Her wide range of business interests includes farming, retailing, restaurants, clothing, spas, and natural wellbeing, and both Daylesford and Bamford have been honored with numerous awards.
"I believe in simple, good food, which is the result of organic farming; it is better for us, our animals, and the environment."

WHAT IS YOUR FAVORITE GREEK FOOD?
Freshly caught sardines grilled on a barbecue, served with lemon and a Greek salad.

IN A FEW WORDS, WHAT DOES GREECE MEAN TO YOU?
I love the simplicity of Greece. The fresh, seasonal food. In particular, spicy olive oil and freshly caught fish. Little chapels perched on cliffs. Greece takes us back to the fundamentals: culture, mathematics, sport, and philosophy.

WHAT IS YOUR FONDEST MEMORY OF GREECE?
The crystal-clear blue sea and a sun-drenched idyllic beach; the white, silvery sand covered with candles. Yoga on the rocks with a backdrop of a beautiful sunset. Memories of Greece are always full of family and friends.

Greek Salad

Χωριάτικη σαλάτα • Horiatiki salata

For a colorful salad, use several varieties of heirloom tomatoes with different shapes and colors. Choose the best Kalamata olives you can find.

Ingredients *(Serves 4)*

- 6 mixed tomatoes
- ¼ cup/60 ml extra-virgin olive oil
- Pinch dried oregano
- Salt and freshly ground black pepper
- 1 cucumber, peeled, quartered lengthwise, seeded, and chopped
- Grated zest and juice of 1 lemon
- 8 oz/250 g feta cheese, crumbled (2 cups)
- 1 small red onion, thinly sliced
- ⅓ cup/60 g Kalamata olives, pitted
- 1 tbsp/15 ml red wine vinegar
- 2 tbsp chopped fresh mint
- 2 tbsp chopped fresh oregano

1 Cut some of the tomatoes into slices and cut the rest in different shapes and sizes to give the salad different textures. Place the tomatoes in a bowl with 2 tablespoons of the oil, add the dried oregano, and season with salt and pepper to taste. Gently toss until well mixed and then place in a colander set over a bowl. Let the tomatoes marinate for a minimum of 15 minutes. (Make sure to keep all the juices from the bowl for the dressing.)

2 Toss the cucumber in a separate large bowl with 1 tablespoon of the oil, half of the lemon zest and juice, and salt and pepper to taste. Add the drained tomatoes, the feta, onion, and olives.

3 Whisk the tomato juice, vinegar, remaining lemon zest and juice, and remaining 2 tablespoons oil together and pour over the salad. Add the fresh mint and oregano leaves, toss, and serve.

i

Cucumbers that have never seen a fridge are much more flavorful and sweeter than the imported ones we get in Britain. To try and recapture this sweetness, I blanch the peeled cucumber in boiling hot water for around 5 seconds and plunge it straight into ice water, again only for 5 seconds, and then I pat it dry with paper towels. This process seems to restore both its color and flavor.

Octopus Carpaccio with Taramosalata & Salad

Χταπόδι καρπάτσιο με ταραμοσαλάτα και σαλάτα
Htapodi carpaccio me taramosalata kai salata

1 *For the octopus carpaccio:* Rinse the octopus well. Using a sharp knife, cut the octopus just below the eyes to remove the hood. Squeeze or cut out the beak and the cartilage on the other side of the beak. Rinse the octopus again and drain it. Place the octopus in a large pot or Dutch oven with the remaining ingredients and add water until the octopus is completely submerged. Bring to a boil, then reduce the heat and cook until tender, 35 to 45 minutes. (The best way to test for tenderness is to insert a sharp knife into the fattest part of the flesh; if the knife passes through with ease it's ready.) Let the octopus cool in the cooking liquid, then drain in a colander. Discard the other ingredients. Place 2 sheets of plastic wrap on the counter, cut the octopus into individual tentacles and place on the plastic wrap. Roll the octopus tentacles into a sausage shape, wrapping tightly in the plastic wrap. Refrigerate for at least 2 hours.

2 *For the taramosalata*: Combine the milk and bread in a small saucepan and warm over low heat, stirring, until the bread has been totally softened and takes on a paste-like form. Let cool, then transfer to a blender. Add the roe and garlic and process until smooth. Slowly add the oil and finish with the lemon juice. Refrigerate for at least 1 hour.

Ingredients *(Serves 4)*

Octopus Carpaccio

* 1 (2-lb/1-kg) octopus
* 5 small tomatoes, halved
* 2 small fennel bulbs, halved
* 1 onion, quartered
* 1 head garlic, left whole
* 2 red chile peppers
* 3 sprigs fresh thyme
* Zest of 1 orange plus 1½ cups/350 ml orange juice

Taramosalata

* ¾ cup/200 ml whole milk
* 2 slices white bread or brioche, crusts removed (about 3½ oz/100 g)
* 3½ oz/100 g white tarama paste (salted cod roe)
* 1 garlic clove, chopped
* 4 tsp extra-virgin olive oil
* Juice of ½ lemon

Salad

* 1 fennel bulb, stalks removed, fronds reserved and chopped, bulb very thinly sliced
* ½ cucumber, peeled, halved lengthwise, and sliced
* 2 tbsp olive oil
* Juice of ½ lemon
* 2 oranges, peeled and segmented
* Fresh dill

3 *To make the salad:* While making the salad, put the fennel bulb and cucumber in ice water to keep them crisp and bring out their flavor. Octopus is best served at room temperature so take it out of the fridge 10 minutes before you dress the salad. Slice the octopus tentacles as finely as possible and arrange on a serving plate. Place a spoonful of taramosalata on each circle of octopus. Remove the cucumber and fennel from the ice water and pat dry with a dish towel. Place in a bowl, sprinkle with the olive oil and lemon juice, and toss to coat. Arrange the cucumber and fennel on top of the octopus, add the orange segments, and sprinkle the dill and fennel fronds over the salad. Finish with any remaining dressing from the fennel and cucumber and serve.

Baked Figs & Custard in Phyllo Pastry

Γαλακτομπούρεκο με σύκα • Galaktoboureko me syka

1 *For the custard:* In a small saucepan, heat the milk to around 185°F/85°C over medium heat. Sift the flour and custard powder into a bowl, add the yolks and sugar, and beat well. Gradually add the warm milk to the egg yolk mixture, whisking constantly. Return to the pan and simmer until thick, around 4 minutes. Remove from the heat, transfer to a clean bowl, cover, and refrigerate until completely cold.

2 *For the pastry:* Preheat the oven to 350°F/180°C. Melt the butter in a small saucepan over low heat. Combine the honey and lemon juice in a second small saucepan and bring just to a boil. Line 2 baking sheets with parchment paper. Place a sheet of phyllo dough on 1 baking sheet and brush generously with butter. Sprinkle some walnuts over the top and then sprinkle lightly with some of the honey and lemon mixture. Repeat the process till you have a stack of 10 sheets of phyllo. Repeat with the remaining phyllo, butter, honey and lemon, and walnuts on the second baking sheet. Bake until the phyllo is golden brown and flaky. Let cool slightly, then, using a sharp serrated knife, cut each phyllo stack into 6 even squares (for a total of 12 pieces).

Ingredients *(Serves 4)*

Custard

* 1 cup plus 3 tbsp/280 ml milk
* 3 tbsp/25 g all-purpose flour
* 2 tbsp Bird's Custard Powder (available online, or use instant vanilla pudding)
* 4 egg yolks
* 7 tbsp/90 g sugar

Pastry

* 8 tbsp/120 g unsalted butter
* 3 tbsp honey
* 2 tbsp lemon juice
* 7 oz/200 g phyllo pastry (about 20 sheets) (see p. 75)
* 1 ¼ cups/150 g chopped walnuts

Figs

* ½ cup/100 g sugar
* 8 ripe figs, halved
* 1 sprig fresh thyme

3 *For the figs:* Pour the sugar into a dry saucepan and cook over moderate heat until the sugar melts and turns a light golden color, stirring constantly as soon as the sugar has started to color. Add the halved figs and cook gently for a couple of minutes until the figs are plump and coated in sugar; add the thyme sprig and remove from the heat. Let cool.

To assemble, whisk the set custard to a smooth consistency. Place four squares of phyllo pastry on individual dessert plates, top each with a spoonful of custard and two fig halves, then repeat with four more phyllo squares, more custard and fig halves, and finally top with the remaining four phyllo squares. 4
Serve.

CAT CORA

Cat Cora made television history in 2005 when she became the first female Iron Chef on Food Network's Iron Chef America. *Since then, she's become a prominent figure in the culinary community and beyond as an accomplished author, restaurateur, contributing editor, television host, avid philanthropist, lifestyle entrepreneur, and proud mother of four.*

Cora grew up in an intimate Greek community in Jackson, Mississippi, where she developed a passion for the culinary arts while watching her family infuse Southern delicacies with Mediterranean spices. As a young adult, she acted on advice from her mentor, Julia Child, and left Mississippi for New York to study at the Culinary Institute of America. She continued her culinary education in Europe before traveling west to Napa Valley, California.

As a successful restaurateur, she has launched a chain of restaurants called Cat Cora's Kitchen as well as Ocean by Cat Cora on Sentosa Island in Singapore. In 2004, Cora founded Chefs for Humanity, a nonprofit dedicated to reducing hunger worldwide by supporting humanitarian relief and promoting nutrition education. In July 2012, she became the first female chef to be inducted into the American Academy of Chefs® Culinary Hall of Fame.

WHAT IS YOUR FAVORITE GREEK FOOD?
I have so many, but I really love the simplest, most ancient native products, the extra-virgin olive oil, cheeses, honey, citrus, the wines—I could go on and on. In fact, I can't think of a Greek food or product I don't love.

IN A FEW WORDS, WHAT DOES GREECE MEAN TO YOU?
It means love of life, spirit of the moment, wonderful foods, people, culture, history, family, and beauty. And more than anything, Greece is about embracing life fully.

WHAT IS YOUR FONDEST MEMORY OF GREECE?
Being there with my whole family when my father and uncle were both still alive. We were there with Food Network for Greek Easter. It was the deepest, most wonderful moment ever.

Stewed Chicken

Κότα καπαμά · Kota kapama

Chicken kapama*, as all the Cora family call it, is one of our favorite traditional dishes. On our birthdays, my brothers and I always got to pick our favorite birthday dinner. I don't remember a single birthday of mine when I did not choose chicken* kapama*. Sometimes I even managed to bribe my younger brother, Chris, to choose it. The best thing about this dish is that you don't have to stand over it. Once everything is stewing, it can be left, with the exception of the occasional stir. The chicken is cut into pieces so that everyone in the family gets their favorite. You can buy the chicken parts that you prefer, dark or light, or you can buy a whole chicken and cut it into pieces. This usually worked out for us since the only big request was from my older brother Mike, who wanted the neck (yuck), and my grandmother, who wanted the back. Believe me, I didn't fight for either of those pieces. Chris and I were always convinced we got the best part, the drumsticks. And if the* kapama *wasn't perfection in itself, the grated* myzithra *(aromatic sheep's cheese), on the side made it even tastier. This cheese was so prized by my parents that we only got it for special occasions. Pecorino or Parmesan are fine subsitutes if you can't get hold of aged* myzithra*. Together, the cheese and the orzo, rice, or noodles that accompany this dish make it magical. (Prepare whichever you choose according to package directions while the chicken is cooking.) This Cora family recipe has been handed down from generation to generation. I hope you enjoy it, too.*

Ingredients *(Serves 4)*

* 1 (2½- to 3-lb/1.2- to 1.4-kg) chicken, cut into 8 pieces
* 1 tsp ground cinnamon
* Coarse salt and freshly ground black pepper
* 2 tbsp olive oil
* 2 yellow onions, coarsely chopped
* 5 garlic cloves, peeled (3 minced, 2 whole)
* ½ cup/120 ml dry white wine
* 1 (6-oz/170-g) can tomato paste
* 1 tbsp chopped fresh oregano
* 1 oz/30 g aged *myzithra*, Parmesan, or pecorino cheese, grated (½ cup)

1. Pat the chicken dry with paper towels. Mix the cinnamon, 2 teaspoons salt, and 1 teaspoon pepper in a small bowl. Rub the chicken pieces on all sides with the seasoning.

2. Heat the oil in a large, deep skillet over high heat. Add the chicken and cook until well browned on both sides, 4 to 5 minutes on each side. Turn the pieces using a spatula or wooden spoon, as they have a tendency to stick to the pan. Don't overcrowd; if necessary, brown the chicken in batches. Transfer the chicken pieces to a plate.

3 Lower the heat to medium-high and add the onions and minced garlic. Cook, stirring constantly, until the onions have softened and are a rich golden brown. Add the wine and scrape the bottom of the pan with a spatula or spoon to deglaze the pan, loosening any particles stuck on the bottom.

4 When the wine has evaporated, add 2 cups water, the tomato paste, oregano, and the whole garlic cloves. Return the chicken to the pan; the pieces should be about three-quarters submerged in the liquid. Cover the pan and simmer until the chicken is tender and thoroughly cooked, about 1 hour. If the sauce becomes too thick, thin it with a little more water. Season the finished sauce with salt and pepper to taste.
Serve the chicken over orzo, rice, or noodles, topped with sauce and sprinkled with *Myzithra*.

CHRIS CHELIOS

Christos Kostas Chelios, of Greek heritage, was born in Chicago, Illinois in 1962. He is one of the most well-known professional hockey players, having played for the Montreal Canadiens, Chicago Blackhawks, Detroit Red Wings, and Atlanta Thrashers for a total of 26 seasons before retiring in 2010. Chelios has held a number of records during his illustrious playing career, including playing the most games as defenseman in National Hockey League history, being the only player to play in over 400 games for three different teams, and having one of the longest careers in the NHL. In 2013 he was inducted into the Hockey Hall of Fame. Chris also represented the United States at four Olympic Winter Games (1984, 1988, 2002, 2006), three Canada Cups (1984, 1987, 1991), two World Cup of Hockey events (1996, 2004), and one World Junior Championship (1982). He is currently the executive advisor to Ken Holland, the general manager of the Detroit Red Wings. Chris lives in the Detroit area with his wife, Tracee, and their four children.

WHAT IS YOUR FAVORITE GREEK FOOD?

I would have to say that three of my most favorite Greek foods are pastitsio (see pp. 102, 129), which is a Greek lasagna, only lighter and much tastier; *avgolemono* (egg-lemon) soup; and lamb chops prepared Greek-style. Of course, I would have to pair all of these meals with Greek Kalamata olives and feta cheese. Oh, and don't forget the bread!

IN A FEW WORDS, WHAT DOES GREECE MEAN TO YOU?

Growing up as the son of an immigrant father and a mother who was born in Chicago but raised in Greece, I was surrounded by the wonderful flavors of Greek food at a very young age. Food is a very big part of Greek family life. Dinnertime always included a lot of traditional Greek dishes and a lot of conversation. It can get very loud at the dinner table of a Greek family and I would have to be sure to let my friends know when they came over to partake in my mom's homemade meals that nobody was mad; it was just the way we communicated. I was never exposed to many of the traditional American dishes that were staples in most households. While all my friends around me were having tacos, pizza, and meatloaf for dinner, I was served *rizaki* (rice), oxtails, and lentils prepared Greek-style. Dinner always included a Greek salad, Greek olives and a super-abundance of bread. My father would make *avgolemono* soup every Sunday and it would be an all-day event. My mother served American favorites such as spaghetti, rice, and chicken but they were always prepared Greek-style, i.e. with a lot of oregano, olive oil, and lemon.

WHAT IS YOUR FONDEST MEMORY OF GREECE?

I have been fortunate to play professional ice hockey for three NHL teams in my career: the Montreal Canadiens, the Chicago Blackhawks, and the Detroit Red Wings. Each of these cities has a large Greek community and many Greek restaurants, so even though I didn't have my mother's home-cooked meals to come home to, I was able to continue to enjoy the healthy foods from my heritage that had become a large part of my daily diet. In other words, I guess you could say my memories of the Greek way of eating are reinforced with almost every meal I ate as a professional athlete, and they are reproduced at home now by my wife, Tracee, who is an excellent cook.

Greek Hamburgers

Μπιφτέκια σχάρας · *Biftekia scharas*

Ingredients *(Serves 4)*

* 3 tbsp olive oil
* 1 large white onion, coarsely grated
* 1 lb/500 g ground beef
* 3 oz/100 g ground lamb
* 1½ cups/70 g fresh breadcrumbs
* 1 tomato, coarsely grated, skin discarded
* 1 roasted red Florina or bell pepper, diced (optional)
* 8 pitted black olives, quartered
* 1 egg, beaten
* 1 tbsp finely chopped fresh parsley
* 1 tbsp mustard
* 1 tsp vinegar
* ¼ tsp garlic powder
* ¼ tsp dried oregano
* Salt and freshly ground black pepper

1 Heat the oil in a large skillet over medium-high heat, add the onion, and cook, stirring until translucent, about 4 minutes. Transfer to a large bowl and let cool completely. Add the beef, lamb, breadcrumbs, tomato, pepper (if using), olives, egg, parsley, mustard, vinegar, garlic powder, and oregano and season with salt and pepper to taste. Mix and knead with your hands until thoroughly blended. Cover and refrigerate for 30 minutes or more.

2 Preheat a gas or charcoal grill (or heat the broiler). Form the meat mixture into either small, thin patties (4⅜ ounces/125 g) or large, thick patties (8 ounces/225 g). Place the patties on the grill and cook to your desired doneness. The length of time will depend on their size; small, thin burgers will take about 3 minutes on each side, while real burgers about an inch thick will need 2 to 3 minutes per side for rare, 3 to 4 minutes for medium, and 4 to 5 for well-done.

i *Serve with warm pita bread or buns with tzatziki and a big mixed green salad.*

Florina peppers are long, bullhorn-shaped sweet peppers grown in northern Greece. You can roast your own or buy them roasted and brined, in jars or cans. Sweet red bell peppers will also work in this recipe.

CHRISTIAN KAREMBEU

Christian Karembeu was born in New Caledonia in 1970. A former top international French football player, he helped secure the FIFA World Cup in 1998, the UEFA European Championship two years later, and in 2001 the FIFA Confederations Cup. In addition, Christian earned other major titles with France, two Champions League titles with Real Madrid, an Intercontinental Cup, and two Greek Championship titles while playing with Olympiacos. Because of his outstanding football achievements, he was named chevalier of the Legion of Honor following the 1998 World Cup, and was twice decorated as Best Player of the Year for the region of Oceania, in 1995 and 1998. After the end of his football career, Christian became a UEFA Ambassador as well as a Strategic Advisor for Olympiacos FC, keeping strong ties with Greece, a country that he deeply loves. He is a member of Champions for Peace, a group of 54 elite athletes committed to serving peace in the world through sport, created by Peace and Sport, a Monaco-based international organization. He is also the host of French travel program on TV.

WHAT IS YOUR FAVORITE GREEK FOOD?

My favorite Greek food? I would say the traditional Greek souvlaki: thin slices of slowly cooked chicken and pork gyros wrapped in pita bread, filled with slices of delicious tomatoes, onions, and the famous Greek tzatziki sauce made of Greek yogurt, cucumber, and garlic. Fried potatoes on the side are an extra bonus. For me this dish is not only a full meal, but also incorporates fine Greek products and unique tastes.

IN A FEW WORDS, WHAT DOES GREECE MEAN TO YOU?

Greece is all about tradition, history, philosophy, and mythology. A magical land of landscapes and islands, beautiful monuments and temples, and people filled with an amazing energy. For me, coming from New Caledonia, the sea represents the continuity of the land and thus of life. This is why the Greek sea has a special place in my heart.

WHAT IS YOUR FONDEST MEMORY OF GREECE?

I have so many memories of this beautiful country that I honestly cannot pick one. Memories coming from my daily life here, from holidays with friends discovering beautiful places, recipes, and local traditions, from my years in Olympiacos and the love I have received from the Greek fans . . . every day something new and special, a land of many gods and goddesses!

Perfect Greek-Style Grilled Fish

Ψάρι ψητό στη σχάρα · Psari psito sti schara

So many of our contributors said their favorite dish was a simple grilled fish, fresh from the sea and still tasting of it, flavor unobscured by sauces or marinades, that we had to include a recipe for it. Greek fish used for this dish include tsipoura *(gilt-head bream),* lavraki *(seabass), and* milokopi *(bearded umbrine). If you cannot find a Mediterranean fish, then a red snapper, pompano, or striped bass might be almost as good. It goes without saying that the fish must be fresh. Grilled fish in Greece are almost always accompanied by a separate bowl of oil and lemon dressing (*ladolemono*), which seems to make them taste even better.*

1 Light a gas or charcoal grill (or heat the broiler).

2 Dry the fish well and brush both sides of each fish with 1 tablespoon of the olive oil. Place the fish on the grill (or under the broiler) and cook for 7 minutes, then flip the fish over and cook for 7 more minutes, until juicy inside and crispy on the outside. (Avoid flipping the fish frequently, as you would with meat. Grilling fish needs a delicate touch.) Grill the tomato halves alongside the fish.

3 *For the olive oil and lemon dressing:* While the fish and tomato are on the grill, mix all the ingredients together. Add the grilled tomato to the dressing and mash with a fork.

4 Place the fish on a big warm platter, sprinkle with chopped parsley, and serve with the dressing.

Ingredients *(Serves 4)*

* 2 (1½-lb/700-g) whole fish, cleaned, scaled, and gutted
* 2 tbsp olive oil
* 1 tomato, sliced in half
* Chopped fresh parsley

Olive Oil and Lemon Dressing

* ½ cup/120 ml olive oil
* Juice of 1 lemon
* 1 tsp brown sugar
* Salt and freshly ground white pepper

i

You can use an instant-read food thermometer to tell when the fish is ready; the ideal temperature in the thickest part of the fish, that is, behind the head, should be about 140°F/60°C. Or just poke it gently with a fork and if the flesh flakes, it's ready.

Homemade Chicken Souvlaki

Σπιτικό σουβλάκι κοτόπουλο μαριναρισμένο
Spitiko souvlaki kotopoulo marinarismeno

Souvlaki, whether on a skewer or cut from a gyro, and with all the trimmings, is an almost universal favorite with young Greeks and tourists. It's usually made with pork, but chicken is a lighter, perhaps healthier option, especially if you use a free-range or organic chicken. With this recipe, you can close your eyes and imagine you're eating on a street in Athens or in an island port in high summer. You will need metal or wooden skewers for this recipe.

Ingredients *(Serves 4)*

Chicken and Marinade

* 2 tbsp mustard
* 1 tbsp finely chopped fresh parsely
* 1 tbsp chopped fresh rosemary
* 1 tsp sweet paprika
* Grated zest of ½ lemon
* 1 garlic clove, crushed
* ½ tsp honey
* Salt and freshly ground black pepper
* 2 boneless, skinless chicken breasts (about 1 lb/500 g total), trimmed and cut into 2-in/5-cm cubes

Trimmings

* 1 onion, layers separated
* 1 large boiled potato, peeled and thinly sliced
* 2 tbsp olive oil
* 4 Greek pita breads (whole wheat if possible)
* 2 romaine lettuce leaves, thinly sliced
* ¼ cup/70 g Greek yogurt or tzatziki
* 4 tomato slices, halved

1 *For the chicken and marinade:* Put the mustard, parsley, rosemary, paprika, lemon zest, garlic, honey, and salt and pepper to taste in a jar and shake well. Place the chicken pieces in a bowl and pour the marinade over them. Cover and refrigerate for at least 2 hours.

2 *For the trimmings:* Light a gas or charcoal grill and get it piping-hot. Slide the chicken cubes onto the skewers with pieces of onion between them. Brush the potato slices lightly with oil. Grill the chicken souvlaki for 3 minutes on each side and grill the potato slices for 1 minute on each side. Grill the pita breads for 2 minutes on each side.

3 Have a platter ready for assembling the souvlaki, with 4 large squares of parchment paper or aluminum foil. Place a hot pita bread on each square. Spread 1 tablespoon of the yogurt on each pita bread, then add some lettuce shreds, 2 half-slices of tomato, and 2 or 3 slices of potato.

Grab 1 pita with the help of the paper or foil, place a chicken skewer in the middle of the pita, and, while squeezing the pita, pull down on the skewer to slide off the chicken cubes and onion into it. (If this sounds authentic and fun but too messy, just slide the chicken off with a fork.) Wrap the lower half of the pita in a big paper napkin. Do the same with the remaining pitas and serve.

i

If you want gyro-style souvlaki, marinate the chicken breasts whole, grill them for 6 to 7 minutes on each side, and then, with a large, sharp knife cut them into very thin slices and assemble the same way.

CHRISTINA HINDS

Christina Hinds is a Greek American former Olympic-level beach volleyball player. She competed for six years on the FIVB tour with the National Team of Greece. In 2012, Christina returned to Los Angeles and became a sought-after lifestyle coach to the stars, curating adventures locally and around the world to discover ways of living at your best. Her company has attracted partnerships with prominent wellness leaders, widening her following and deepening her experiences. As an expert traveler and athlete, Christina now consults for various travel and healthy lifestyle companies, enhancing their holistic perspectives. She has a B.A. in psychology from Pepperdine University and an Integrative Nutrition Degree from IIN (Institute for Integrative Nutrition) in New York City.

WHAT IS YOUR FAVORITE GREEK FOOD?

My favorite Greek food is my *yiayia's* (grandma's) *dolmadakia*, grape leaves fresh from the garden stuffed with rice and meat and served warm with olive oil and homemade Greek yogurt to dip. Because they are bite-size I eat them like popcorn. We always make a lot of them because they are just as good the next day as when they are fresh out of the pot. To be honest, I love all Greek food.

IN A FEW WORDS, WHAT DOES GREECE MEAN TO YOU?

As an athlete, I feel my Greek blood pulse in the toughest of battles . . . an ancient knowledge, a strong heart, a rich soul, and a free spirit.

WHAT IS YOUR FONDEST MEMORY OF GREECE?

Although a decadent life in Greece is almost indescribably glorious, it's the simple life Greece highlights that stands out the most in my mind.

It's the sardines fresh out of the sea, which most people consider bait, with rich Kalamata olive oil and fresh lemon squeezed all over them, along with a cold glass of ouzo shared in a charming, dirty little underground garage with my father and his friends singing at the tops of their lungs, eyes closed, genuine smiles, hands waving above their heads, dancing to the classic sounds of *rebetiko* (Greek blues), during a time of dire crisis in Greece. It's this relentless spirit of joy in tough moments that touches me the most about Greece and Hellenes in general.

It's waking up in a deserted cove after a warm night of sailing. Diving into the deepening blues of the open sea and smiling at the wonder of the world. The sea in Greece breathes and whispers like nowhere I've ever been before. The intense colors and smooth texture arouse my senses and calm me simultaneously.

It's my happy place. With my father, I spend the morning fishing and catching our lunch. We traditionally lunch at the beach with only a knife, a spoon, and lemon. He heats up stones under the hot summer sun and sears our octopus and fish to perfection, while I crack open our sea urchins for appetizers.

We look at each other and laugh as we eat like kings and queens with a view of heaven on earth, witnessed only by the gods.

Smyrna Sausages

Σουτζουκάκια · Soutzoukakia

These spicy "sausages" (really more like meatballs), with their rich, cumin-flavored tomato sauce, are among the most popular dishes brought to Greece by the refugees from Asia Minor in the 1920s. Many of them arrived with only the clothes they were wearing, their recipes, and their music, but they had a tremendous influence on the culture and cuisine of their new home. These sausages go beautifully with fried potatoes or rice pilaf. If you don't have red wine on hand, you can use a half-and-half combination of water and vinegar to soak the bread.

Ingredients *(Serves 6 to 8)*

* ½ loaf day-old Italian or Greek "peasant" bread, crusts removed
* ½ cup/120 ml red wine or ¼ cup/60 ml vinegar and ¼ cup/60 ml water
* 2 lb/1 kg ground beef
* 1 onion, grated
* 3 garlic cloves, finely chopped
* 2 tsp ground cumin
* Salt and freshly ground black pepper
* ½ cup/120 ml olive oil

Sauce

* 2 lb/1 kg fresh tomatoes, halved, grated, skins discarded, or 1 (28-oz/800-g) can whole tomatoes, crushed
* 1 onion, grated
* 2 garlic cloves, crushed
* 1 tsp sugar (optional)
* 1 piece dried orange peel (optional)
* 2 tsp ground cumin, or to taste
* Salt and freshly ground black pepper

1. Crumble the bread and soak it in the wine (or vinegar/water solution) for 30 minutes. Squeeze out all the liquid with your hands, then add the beef, onion, garlic, and cumin and season with salt and pepper. Knead the mixture together. Make fattish "sausages" about 3 inches/7 cm long and 2 inches/5 cm wide (they should taper into round points at the ends) and refrigerate for at least an hour or until ready to cook. Heat the oil in a large skillet over medium-high heat, and fry the sausages until cooked through. Drain on paper towels and set aside. Reserve the frying oil.

2. *For the sauce:* Combine the tomatoes, onion, garlic, sugar (if using), and orange peel (if using) in a medium saucepan and bring to a boil. Reduce the heat and simmer until the sauce is nice and thick. Add the cumin and salt and pepper to taste and cook for another minute or two.

3. Ten minutes before you're ready to eat, add the sausages to the sauce along with a few tablespoons of the reserved frying oil and simmer to blend the flavors, adding a little water or red wine if needed. Serve.

COSTA PILAVACHI

Born in London and raised primarily in Canada, the United States, and Greece, Costa Pilavachi has worked in classical music all his life. Starting his career in Ottawa and Toronto, he was the artistic administrator of the Boston Symphony Orchestra under Seiji Ozawa before joining the record industry at Philips Classics in The Netherlands. Over the years, as president of Decca and EMI Classics and now as senior vice president of Universal Music Group International, the world's leading music company, Costa advises, signs, develops, and works with emerging and celebrated artists from every continent, and is a consultant to many top musicians and organizations. He is also a passionate sailor and an excellent cook.

WHAT IS YOUR FAVORITE GREEK FOOD?

Lamb fricassee with curly endives and *avgolemono* sauce. Yum.

IN A FEW WORDS, WHAT DOES GREECE MEAN TO YOU?

Greece is my fantasy that comes true. I have spent almost my entire life abroad dreaming of long, hot summers in the islands. Now I am able to go more often and it is a thrill, every time. I am happiest in Greece, summer or winter. It is the light, the food, the closeness to nature, the incredible spirit of the people, the sense of humor.

WHAT IS YOUR FONDEST MEMORY OF GREECE?

There are so many happy memories, but the summers spent in Spetses in the 1960s, sailing with my cousins, dancing barefoot in the Blueberry Hill disco, and cycling all around the island are absolutely unforgettable.

Liz's Watermelon Gazpacho

Το γκασπάτσο της Λιζ με καρπούζι · To gaspacho tis Liz me karpouzi

My wife, Liz, likes any raw soups to be easy on the digestion so she avoids all the hearty stuff like raw green peppers or raw red onion or garlic, which seem to go in most recipes of this kind. She finds that having a tasty variety of the basic ingredients is much more important and allows you to make a very delicious gazpacho with very little fuss. Personally, I love to serve watermelon gazpacho as an amuse-bouche *in espresso cups together with other snacks; people always come back for seconds or thirds. Choose a small watermelon, preferably seedless, with a dark green rind and deep red flesh. This type of watermelon has a richer flavor and a round sweetness, which is what you need to counterbalance the acidity in the tomatoes. For the tomatoes, the large beefsteak variety works best; choose very ripe tomatoes and make sure to remove the seeds.*

Ingredients

* 6 cups/920 g watermelon, peeled, seeded, and chopped
* 2 cups/400 g tomatoes, peeled, seeded, and chopped
* 1 cucumber, peeled, seeded, and finely diced
* 2 tbsp garlic-infused olive oil
* Juice of 1 lemon or lime (I use both together, half and half)
* ½ tsp ground cumin (optional)
* Sea salt and freshly ground black pepper
* Small bunch fresh parsley stems, finely chopped
* Small bunch fresh cilantro stems, finely chopped
* Handful fresh mint leaves, finely chopped
* Tabasco

1 Working in batches, puree the watermelon and tomato in a blender until smooth and transfer to a large bowl. Add the cucumber, garlic-infused olive oil, citrus juice, cumin (if using), and salt to taste. Stir to combine. Combine the parsley and cilantro stems and mint leaves in a small bowl.

2 To serve, divide the gazpacho into bowls. Add a dash of Tabasco and a few grinds of pepper to each, and then top with a scoop of the finely chopped herbs.

i *If you prefer a smooth soup, puree the cucumber together with the tomatoes in the blender.*

Seafood Risotto

Ριζότο με θαλασσινά · Risoto me thalassina

This risotto tastes best with a mixture of different kinds of seafood, and any firm skinless and boneless white fish fillet can be used in place of one of the seafood varieties listed below. The fish broth should not be too strongly flavored; a 50-50 mix of water and broth is fine. If you can get fresh fish broth, use it; otherwise, canned or reconstituted broth is acceptable.

1 Bring the broth to a simmer in a small saucepan and keep warm.

2 Heat some of the oil in a large skillet over medium-high heat, add some of the seafood (don't crowd the pan), and fry for about 1 minute. The seafood should be slightly undercooked but not raw. Transfer to a bowl and repeat with the remaining oil and seafood, working in batches. Reserve any residual liquids.

3 Melt the butter in a large, heavy-bottomed pot or Dutch oven over medium heat. Add the onion and cook, stirring with a wooden spoon, until soft and translucent. (Do not burn.) Add the rice and stir constantly until the grains are well coated with butter, 1 to 1½ minutes. Add the white wine and stir constantly until almost absorbed.

4 Add a ladleful of the hot broth (about ⅔ cup/100 ml) and cook, stirring constantly, making sure nothing is sticking to the sides or bottom of the pot. When this liquid has been absorbed but the rice is still wet, repeat this process until you have used all the broth, 20 to 25 minutes.

Ingredients *(Serves 4 as a main course or 6 as an appetizer)*

- 5 cups/1.2 L fish broth
- 3½ tbsp/50 ml olive oil
- 2 lb/1 kg seafood such as squid, octopus, shrimp, and clams, cleaned and cut into ½-in/1.5-cm pieces
- 4 tbsp/55 g unsalted butter
- ½ cup/70 g finely chopped onion
- 2¼ cups/450 g arborio or carnaroli rice
- ¼ cup/60 ml dry white wine
- ¼ cup/20 g chopped fresh parsley
- 1½ oz/50 g Parmesan cheese, grated (¾ cup) (optional)
- Sea salt and freshly ground white pepper

5 When you feel that the risotto is almost fully cooked, add the seafood with any reserved liquid and the parsley. Continue to cook, stirring, for about 2 minutes.

6 Once you are satisfied with the risotto's consistency, remove it from the heat and add the Parmesan (if using). Season with salt and pepper to taste (you may find that the seafood and Parmesan, if used, have provided enough salt), cover, and let the risotto rest for a few minutes before serving.

Bubbly Zabaglione

Κρέμα ζαμπαγιόνε με σαμπάνια · Krema zabaglione me sampania

This is a more festive, effervescent version of the Italian classic and although it is just as rich, it feels lighter.

1 Divide the strawberries among 4 to 6 dessert bowls.

2 Combine the egg yolks and sugar in a heatproof bowl and set it over a saucepan filled with about 1 inch/2.5 cm of simmering water. (The bowl should not touch the water.) Whisk until foamy. Slowly add the champagne and whisk constantly until the mixture is thick and creamy, about 10 minutes.

3 Remove from heat, add the kirsch and serve immediately over the berries.

Ingredients *(Serves 4 to 6)*

- 1 lb/500 g strawberries, hulled, large berries cut in half, small ones left whole
- 4 egg yolks
- ⅓ cup/65 g sugar
- ¾ cup/180 ml champagne or good sparkling wine, at room temperature
- 2 tbsp kirsch, cognac, or other fruit brandies

DAN & DEAN CATEN

Born in Canada in 1964, Dean and Dan Catenacci are the youngest of nine children. In love with fashion from an early age, the twin brothers began their careers by designing outfits for their older sisters. After studying at Parson's School of Design and working in New York, the pair moved to Milan in 1991 to pursue a new fashion adventure in Italy. Their debut men's collection in 1995 was a runway success, and set the template for their brand Dsquared2. Dan and Dean Caten's vision for Dsquared2 broke the mold of a traditional luxury fashion brand. It is fun, sexy, glamorous and irreverent, accidentally chic and uncontrived cool. Branching out into women's and kids' clothing, as well as eyewear and underwear, Dan and Dean Caten have received numerous fashion awards. They were named official designers for the opening and closing ceremonies for the Vancouver Olympics in 2010, received a star on Toronto's Walk of Fame in 2009, and garnered a CAFA Outstanding Achievement Award in 2014. The designers are also active supporters of charities AMFAR and Fashion Cares.

WHAT IS YOUR FAVORITE GREEK FOOD?
That's a hard question because all Greek food is special and delicious. But if we had to choose, we'd pick the typical salad with feta cheese. It's the perfect dish to eat on a hot day at the beach. When we want to indulge our sweet tooth, we love *kataifi*, one of our favorite desserts. But we're also obsessed with *tiropites*, those delicious triangles filled with cheese, while *spanakopita* (see pp. 97, 142)— spinach pie—is certainly also a great dish, filling but very healthy and probably among our favorites. Of course, when thinking of Greece, it's difficult not to mention the olives, the wine, the cheese, the fresh fish . . . Greece is everything, it has a special and unique "sound!"

IN A FEW WORDS, WHAT DOES GREECE MEAN TO YOU?
To us, Greece, or more specifically Mykonos, is almost like a second home. We go to Mykonos at least once a year with all of our friends and family, and some of our best memories are from there. We know the town, the people are so warm, the beaches are amazing. That island, with its colors and smells, always makes us feel welcome and at home. It's a place where we can relax, enjoy ourselves, and kick back. Now that we have opened our boutique in Mykonos it gives us a great reason to travel there more often. We love the way Mykonos always welcomes us!

WHAT IS YOUR FONDEST MEMORY OF GREECE?
The opening of our Mykonos boutique is certainly a very special memory. After so many years of traveling there, vacationing and enjoying every little corner of the island, it was a source of great pleasure and pride to open our store in a place that we cherish so much.

Kataifi Nests
with Ice Cream & Morello Cherry Spoon Sweet

Φωλιές με κανταΐφι με παγωτό και γλυκό του κουταλιού βύσσινο
Folies me kataifi me pagoto kai glyko tou koutaliou vissino

Kataifi *is sometimes referred to as shredded wheat pastry. Like phyllo dough, kataifi dough is sold frozen in boxes. Thin, maybe thinner than angel hair pasta, it's commonly formed into syrup-soaked cylinders studded with chopped walnuts. This dessert, which marries the crunch of the pastry with smooth ice cream and the tang of sour cherries, is not as overpoweringly sweet.*

1 Preheat the oven to 325°F/160°C.

2 *For the syrup:* Combine all the ingredients in a small saucepan and simmer over low heat for 7 minutes. Set aside to cool.

3 Separate the *kataifi* into 12 equal parts and place each part in the cup of a muffin tin. Cover the bottoms evenly with the *kataifi* and raise the threads up the sides a little to make nests. Brush them with the melted butter. Bake the nests until they turn a nice dark gold, about 30 minutes. Douse them with the cool syrup, a spoonful at a time. Let cool. Remove the nests from the muffin tin, fill each one with a spoonful of ice cream, and top with some cherry spoon sweet. Serve.

Ingredients *(Serves 12)*

Syrup
* 1 cup/240 ml water
* 1 cup/200 g sugar
* 1 tbsp corn syrup
* 1 cinnamon stick
* 1 strip lemon zest plus 1 tbsp lemon juice

* 8 oz/250 g *kataifi* dough (½ package)
* 8 tbsp/100 g unsalted butter, melted

* Ice cream
* 2 tbsp Morello Cherry Spoon Sweet (see p. 88) per serving

i

If you prefer, you can use 8 ounces/250 g honey in place of the syrup. Warm the honey in a small saucepan over medium heat. As soon as it starts to simmer, remove it from the heat and spoon it over each kataifi *nest. In Greece, we would serve this with* kaimaki *ice cream, which is flavored with* mastiha, *the crystallized resin from the* Pistachia lentiscus *tree, also known as gum Arabic or the tears of Chios, which gives the ice cream a slightly chewy texture.*

DEAN KARNAZES

Runner, writer, surfer, fitness freak, explorer, Dean Karnazes is "drinking from a fountain that's pouring like an avalanche coming down the mountain." Known as the Ultra Marathon Man, after running 50 marathons in 50 states in 50 days, he has also written books and is president of his Good Health Natural Foods company. Hailed by Time *magazine as one of the 100 most influential people in the world as well as one of the fittest, he heads a charity that fights childhood obesity called Karno Kids. At the same time, Dean is uniquely able to demonstrate how the lessons learned from athletics can be applied to business—and has worked for several Fortune 500 companies and start-ups.*

WHAT IS YOUR FAVORITE GREEK FOOD?

Fresh fish. I love Greek foods from the sea.

IN A FEW WORDS, WHAT DOES GREECE MEAN TO YOU?

Arête. Harmony of mind, body, and spirit.

WHAT IS YOUR FONDEST MEMORY OF GREECE?

Swimming near the island of Ikaria, the birthplace of my mother's family.

Not Your Grandmother's Quiche

Τάρτα λαχανικών με κινόα · *Tarta lachanikon me kinoa*

Ingredients *(Serves 6)*

* ½ spaghetti squash, seeds removed
* 1 tbsp coconut oil
* ½ sweet onion, diced
* 1 cup/30 g baby spinach
* 1 cup/185 g cooked quinoa
* ¼ cup/30 g sliced sun-dried tomatoes
* 4 eggs, beaten
* Pinch cayenne pepper
* Coarse sea salt and freshly ground pepper

1. Preheat the oven to 375°F/190°C.

2. Place the squash cut-side down on a baking sheet and bake until tender, 40 to 45 minutes. While the squash is baking, heat the coconut oil in a medium skillet over medium heat. Add the onion and cook, stirring, until translucent. Add the spinach and cook for 2 minutes. Let cool. Reduce the oven temperature to 325°F/160°C.

3. Using a fork, scrape the spaghetti squash flesh into a bowl. Add the spinach and onion mixture, the quinoa, and the tomatoes and mix together. Add the beaten eggs, cayenne, and salt and pepper to taste; stir gently. Scrape the mixture into a 9-inch/23-cm pie plate and bake until a knife inserted in the center comes out clean, about 30 minutes. Let cool slightly, slice into wedges, pound your chest several times while hooting, "AROO! AROO! AROO! "and grind away.

Roasted Fennel

Καραμελωμένος μάραθος στο φούρνο · Karamelomenos marathos sto fourno

"Marathon" is the Greek word for fennel, which happens to grow in abundance along that famous plain. Fresh fennel tastes like a cross between celery and licorice. Roasting, however, brings out an entirely new flavor, as if pine nuts decided to join the party. Here is a very simple, yet delicious, recipe for preparing this underrated vegetable. Use Aegean sea salt here if you can find it.

1. Preheat the oven to 400°F/200°C. Line a baking sheet with aluminum foil.
2. Place the fennel in a bowl, add the olive oil, and stir to coat. Sprinkle vinegar over the fennel and stir to coat. Season with salt to taste. Spread the fennel out evenly over the baking sheet and roast until the fennel begins to caramelize, 30 to 40 minutes. Serve.

Ingredients *(Serves 4 as an appetizer)*

- 2 big fennel bulbs, stalks removed, bulbs halved lengthwise, then cut lengthwise in ½-in/12-mm-thick slices
- 1 tbsp organic olive oil
- Aged balsamic vinegar
- Sea salt

Baklava Blitzer

Μπακλαβάς στο ποτήρι · Baklavas sto potiri

This recipe takes the flavors of baklava and turns them into a healthy drink.

1. Place all the ingredients in a blender and blend on high until frothy and creamy. Serve. *OPA!*

Ingredients *(Serves 1)*

- ¾ cup/180 ml nonfat buttermilk
- ½ cup/140 g Greek yogurt
- 1 tbsp honey
- 1½ tsp chopped pistachios
- 1½ tsp chopped walnuts
- 1 tsp fresh lemon juice
- ½ cup ice cubes

DIANA FARR LOUIS

Diana was born in New York City and grew up on Long Island but didn't feel at home until she discovered Greece in the '60s. Passionate about her adopted country, she explored almost every corner of it by car, on foot, and in a sailboat, and eventually began to write about it, in guidebooks, travel stories over 10 years for the Athens News, *and two cookbooks,* Prospero's Kitchen: Island Cooking of Greece *and* Feasting and Fasting in Crete. *She is also the author of* The Secrets of the Greek Islands, Athens and Beyond, Travels in Northern Greece, *and countless articles, some of which have appeared in* The Huffington Post. *She is a regular contributor to CulinaryBackstreets.com.*

WHAT IS YOUR FAVORITE GREEK FOOD?

Almost anything that comes from the sea, from tiny fried *atherina*, baby *kalamarakia*, fat mussels, and bearded red mullet to octopus, shrimp, and bigger fish, grilled, poached, or made into soup. The simpler the better. But I have to add that to me Greek food is soul food.

IN A FEW WORDS, WHAT DOES GREECE MEAN TO YOU?

Greece is where my heart is. I love its layers of history and the way it intertwines with myth so that on a hike you may find a sign for Hercules's funeral pyre or Odysseus's palace. The extreme beauty of its islands, olive groves, and mountains never fails to move me, but so do the wildflowers—anemones in late winter, cyclamen in the fall; the smells, whether of cooking or of trampled herbs in the countryside and orange blossoms in central Athens; the sounds—sheepbells in the hills, caiques heading out to sea, the shouts (sometimes "rude," sometimes lewd) in the farmers' markets, someone playing a flute next to the Roman Agora. Most of all I'm drawn to the people, whether they're in good spirits and enjoying life to the hilt or down in the dumps and shrugging their shoulders, repeating their mantra, *"Ti na kanoume?"* ("What can we do?") And the way they just get on with it, stoically and creatively. This is a crazy, infuriating, heart-rending place, and wherever you go, it wounds you, as Seferis said. But when you're not there, you ache to be back. Maybe because of its contradictions, it fosters deep friendships as well as spontaneous connections, and these keep us going even in tough times like the present.

WHAT IS YOUR FONDEST MEMORY OF GREECE?

How could I condense 50-plus years into a single memory? Would it be the first time I heard the expression "joy of God day" on a crystal-clear October morning on Spetses; being caught almost at the top of Olympus in a hailstorm with Zeus's tympani crashing around me; sitting in the kitchen listening to the stories told by Eleni, my sister-in-law's cook, who'd been with the family since 1920; swimming with a monk seal off Alonissos; visits to the remote islands of Elafonissos, Pserimos, Kastellorizo, and the Koufonisia before they were "discovered"; experiencing overwhelming hospitality and generosity in Crete while tracking down recipes; being welcomed by the whole neighborhood in Maroussi when my son and I arrived on June 4, 1972, to move into the empty family house. . .? Hardly a day goes by without something memorable happening, even if it's a small thing like spotting a hoopoe or a bee orchid, exchanging a joke or a gripe with the greengrocer, running into a friend in an unlikely spot, or catching sight of the Acropolis framed by city streets, TV aerials, and solar heaters.

Eggplant Smothered in Garlic

Μελιτζάνες σκορδοστούμπι · Melitzanes skordostoumbi

This is my favorite dish from Prospero's Kitchen. *The recipe is from Zakynthos and really belongs to my co-author, June Marinos. It is so delicious that there never seems to be enough and it really should be cooked a day ahead, or at least several hours before you intend to serve it, because it is much much better when it has had time to rest and absorb all the flavors. Resist the temptation to serve it hot, right out of the oven. This goes well with fresh sourdough bread, feta, and plenty of wine.*

Ingredients *(Serves 4 to 8)*

* 4 lb/2 kg large round eggplants, unpeeled, and cut in 1-in/2 ½-cm slices
* Salt and freshly ground black pepper
* Olive oil for frying
* 4 lb/2 kg ripe tomatoes, peeled, halved, seeded, and grated, or 2 lb/1 kg canned tomatoes
* ½ tsp sugar
* 2–3 tbsp vinegar or sweet red wine like Mavrodaphne
* 1 head garlic, peeled and chopped

1 Sprinkle the eggplant slices with salt and leave them in a colander for at least 40 minutes to shed some of their liquid. Rinse and dry the slices well. Heat about an inch of olive oil in a large skillet over medium heat and gently fry the eggplant slices on both sides in batches. Drain on paper towels.

2 Preheat the oven to 375°F/190°C.

3 Place the tomatoes, sugar, and salt and pepper to taste in a large saucepan and simmer until a thickish sauce forms. Stir in the vinegar. Arrange the eggplant slices in layers in an ovenproof dish, sprinkling chopped garlic between each layer. Pour the tomato sauce over the eggplant and bake for 30 minutes. Leave in the oven to cool and serve several hours later or the next day.

i *You can also brush the eggplant slices with oil and grill them for a lighter dish.*

Greek Meatballs

Κεφτεδάκια · Keftedakia

The word keftedes *comes from the classical Persian* kofta *(from* kõftan, *to grind) and little meatballs exist in every culture, but these, with their light, moist interior and crispy crust, are as close as I can come to the ones Eleni used to make for Spetses lunches or cocktail parties on my sister-in-law's terrace. Originally from Ikaria, Eleni inspired adoration for her unbeatable cooking and her tender manner. She used to call us all* chryso mou *(my golden one) and never looked hot, exasperated, or tired even though she spent long hours in the kitchen and never seemed to sit down. She used to chop onions and tomatoes in the palms of her hands, couldn't be bothered with cutting boards, and never left a dish to stew on its own, untended. As Eleni calmly composed her ingredients, it was obvious that the most important was intangible.* Agape, *or love, permeated every dish, which is why they're so difficult to replicate. As she told me, "You can't just toss things into a pan and then leave and go make the beds. You must keep watch. Be attentive. Look after your food till it's ready."*

1 Soak the bread in the wine and squeeze dry. Place in a large bowl and add the beef, onion, egg, parsley, mint, oregano, oil, garlic, and salt and pepper to taste. Mix all the ingredients together with your hands and knead them until well blended and fairly smooth. Set in the refrigerator for an hour or so to let the flavors develop.

2 To make the meatballs, pick off a walnut-sized piece (about 1 tablespoon) of the mixture and roll it in your hands. Place each one on a plate (or in a paper bag) and dredge them with flour.

3 Heat an inch of oil in a large frying pan over medium heat and fry the meatballs in batches until browned on all sides. Do not overcrowd. Drain them on paper towels, and then and this is one of Eleni's secrets—briefly fry them again. (This is what she also did with the fried potatoes that go so well with *keftedakia*.) Frying them twice makes them extra crunchy and ensures that they're cooked through. Serve.

Ingredients

(Makes about 25 meatballs)

* 8 oz/250 g "day-old" bread, crusts removed
* ½ cup, 125 ml wine, red or white, whatever you have open
* 1 pound/500 g ground beef, or a mixture of beef and pork
* 1 onion, grated
* 1 egg, beaten
* 3 tbsp finely chopped fresh parsley
* 3 tbsp finely chopped fresh mint
* 1 tbsp dried oregano
* 1 tbsp olive oil, plus extra for frying
* 1–2 garlic cloves, finely chopped
* Salt and freshly ground black pepper
* All-purpose flour for dredging

i

Baking these meatballs on a baking sheet in a hot oven (400°F/200°C) is also a less messy and probably healthier option. When I do that, I omit the flour and shake a drop of soy sauce on each ball. Turn halfway through the cooking time of 15 to 20 minutes.

Raisin Cake

Σταφιδόπιτα · Stafidopita

This is my favorite recipe from Feasting and Fasting in Crete. *It comes from Siteia, the raisin capital of Greece. The cake has a toffee-like crunchiness on the outside, while the inside reminds me of old-fashioned wedding cake, though it's moister and even more succulent. Having been invented to perk up fasting periods, this cake contains no eggs or milk but uses extra-virgin olive oil for shortening. It makes a scrumptious snack for winter afternoons and evenings. Leftovers can be turned into delicious rusks for dunking into coffee or tea. Leave the cake a day or two, cut it into neat pieces, and bake them in a low oven for an hour or so until they are hard. They will keep indefinitely.*

1 Preheat the oven to 375°F/190°C. Lightly oil a 9½-inch/24-cm springform pan.

2 Soak the raisins in the brandy for about 10 minutes and then chop them in a food processor. Stir the baking soda into the orange juice. Sift the flour, cinnamon, and cloves together into a bowl. In a separate, larger bowl, beat together the oil and sugar until creamy, and slowly add the orange juice and zest, soda water, walnuts, and brandy-soaked raisins. Stir in the flour, a little at a time, until you have a thick batter. Pour into the prepared pan and bake until a sharp knife inserted into the cake comes out clean, about 1 hour. Let cool before you remove it from the pan. Serve.

Ingredients *(Serves 4)*

* 2 cups/300 g golden raisins
* ¼ cup/60 ml raki or brandy
* 1 tbsp baking soda
* Grated zest of 1 orange plus ½ cup/120 ml orange juice
* 3 cups/430 g all-purpose flour
* 1 tsp ground cinnamon
* ½ tsp ground cloves
* 1 cup/240 ml extra-virgin olive oil
* 1 cup/200 g sugar
* ½ cup/120 ml soda water
* 1 cup/150 g chopped walnuts

DIANE KOCHILAS

Celebrity chef, award-winning cookbook author, and cooking school owner Diane Kochilas has been at the forefront of bringing healthy, delicious Greek cuisine to a wide international audience for many years. Every summer, she runs the Glorious Greek Cooking School on her native island, Ikaria. She is consulting chef to several high-profile Greek restaurants in the United States, and is the author of 18 books on Greek and Mediterranean cuisine, including Ikaria: Lessons on Food, Life, and Longevity from the Greek Island Where People Forget to Die; The Country Cooking of Greece, *one of the* New York Times' *100 best books of 2012; and* The Glorious Foods of Greece, *which won the prestigious IACP Jane Grigson prize for excellence in research. In Greece, she hosted a popular TV cooking show,* What Are We Going to Eat Today, Mom? *(in Greek) and was a regular columnist for its largest daily paper,* Ta Nea. *Besides appearing on many major American television shows, she has worked with several universities across the United States to bring healthy Greek cuisine to student dining. Diane divides her time between New York City, the Greek island of Ikaria, and Athens.*

WHAT IS YOUR FAVORITE GREEK FOOD?

I don't have just one favorite Greek food because the cuisine is all about seasonality, and after 23 years here, I have learned to anticipate the bounty of the seasons. Figs and the dark, sweet Fokiano grapes from Ikaria in August. Red Florina peppers, which I grill and put up in olive oil with rosemary and garlic in September. Pumpkins, for pies both savory and sweet in October. Fresh, peppery olive oil in November. The sweets of Christmas, the *melomakárona*, the *kourambiedes*, the honey-doused dough fritters we call *xerotigana* on Ikaria. Delicious crisp cabbages at the height of winter and the cabbage *dolmades* and sharp, spicy salads that we make with them. Greens, greens, greens, from November to May and beyond, boiled simply and served with sea salt we collect from Ikaria, great olive oil, and a little lemon. Fresh tender grape leaves, to freeze, and brine or to roll up fresh with the bounty of spring herbs, especially wild fennel. Greek cherries and apricots. Greek peaches. And, maybe the best thing of all: Greek tomatoes, warm and straight off the vine. When they're married with pungent, aromatic Ikarian oregano, olive oil, real feta, all of which necessitates a slice of old-fashioned bread, then you've got the best of Greece: essential flavors, essential food, seasonal, simple, authentic.

IN A FEW WORDS, WHAT DOES GREECE MEAN TO YOU?

Mana (Mother). Light. Water. Salt. Rocks. Pine. Dust. Honey. Violins. Dance trance. *Filotimo* (Honor). Eroticism. Life. God. Greece, its nature, its energy; I don't really know what it is, but it has something pure that connects us to life instead of shielding us from life, which is what happens in the United States, where I grew up. Greece enables us to be essential and raw, stripped of pretenses, which is ironic because there is also so much ego, so much huffing and puffing here. But there's a depth, an authenticity, which is part of every day's experience. The human experience is deeper here than it is anywhere else I've ever lived or visited.

WHAT IS YOUR FONDEST MEMORY OF GREECE?

The first time I saw the Milky Way in a night sky on Ikaria, far from city lights. The first time I saw shooting stars in August. The first time I stepped into the Aegean and was shocked that I could see my toes. The first whiff I ever got of a garden tomato and the courage I mustered to overcome a 12-year-old's fear and bite into a soft, ripe fig. The first time and every time I dance the *Kariotiko*, carried into something akin to a trance by the violin or the *gaida* (bagpipes). The first time I stayed up all night to dance that *Kariotiko*, then walked home through pine forests on dusty roads on Ikaria, circa 1975, intoxicated by those smells: pine, dust, honey, jasmine, sea brine.

Octopus with Eggplant from Epanomi

Χταπόδι με μελιτζάνες από την Επανομή
Htapodi me melitzanes apo tin Epanomi

1 Soak the octopus for a few minutes in warm water and the vinegar. Rinse well. Using a sharp knife, cut the octopus just below the eyes to remove the hood. Squeeze or cut out the beak and cartilage on the other side of the beak. Rinse and drain the octopus.

2 Place the octopus in a large pot with enough water to cover. Add the allspice and bay leaves. Bring to a boil and simmer until somewhat tender but still firm to the touch, 40 to 50 minutes. Remove, reserving the cooking liquid, let cool slightly, and cut into eight pieces along the tentacles.

3 While the octopus is simmering, preheat the oven to 350°F/180°C.

4 Heat the oil in a large, heavy skillet over medium heat, add the eggplant, and cook, stirring, for a few minutes, until al dente. Remove the eggplant from the skillet with a slotted spoon and set aside. Add the grated tomatoes to the skillet and cook over medium heat until most of their liquid has cooked off and the sauce is thick. Remove from the heat. Toss the eggplant, tomato mixture, and octopus together in a 9 by 13-inch/ 23 x 33-cm baking pan. Season with salt and pepper (go easy on the salt, as the octopus is already salty) and add ½ cup/120 ml of the reserved octopus cooking liquid.

Ingredients

(Serves 4 as a main course or 8 as an appetizer)

* 1 (3-lb/1.35-kg) octopus
* ½ cup/120 ml red wine vinegar
* 5–8 allspice berries
* 3 bay leaves
* 1 cup/240 ml extra-virgin Greek olive oil, plus extra for drizzling
* 3 long eggplants, unpeeled, cut into ¾ in/1.8 cm rounds
* 4 large tomatoes, peeled, seeded, and grated
* Salt and freshly ground black pepper

Drizzle with olive oil and bake uncovered for about 25 minutes or until the liquid has been absorbed and the eggplant and octopus are fork tender.

Adapted from The Country Cooking of Greece *(Chronicle Books, 2012)*

Basic Homemade Phyllo Dough

Σπιτικό φύλλο · Spitiko fyllo

There are about as many recipes for homemade phyllo as there are regional cooks in Greece. The recipe below for homemade phyllo is my basic, all-purpose recipe. It makes a malleable dough that is easy to work with and easy to roll. You can halve the recipe (and, by extension, individual pie and filling proportions) to make smaller pies in 8-in/20-cm or 10-in/25-cm round baking pans. Use this recipe for the Summer Greens Pie with Zucchini and Herbs (see p. 76).

Ingredients *(Makes enough for one 15- to 18-inch/38- to 46-cm pie)*

* 3½–4½ cups/550 g–700 g bread flour or finely ground semolina flour
* 1 scant tsp salt
* 1¼ cups/300 ml water
* ½ cup/120 ml extra-virgin Greek olive oil
* 1 tbsp red wine vinegar, balsamic vinegar, ouzo, or lemon juice

1 In the bowl of a mixer fitted with a dough hook, combine 3¼ cups/510 g of the flour and the salt and mix for about 5 seconds. Add the water, olive oil, and vinegar and mix on low speed for 3 minutes to combine. Increase the speed to medium and knead until the dough is very smooth and pliant and balls up easily, stopping the mixer to add additional flour as needed, ¼ cup/40 grams at a time. The whole mixing process should take about 10 to 12 minutes.

2 Transfer the dough to an oiled bowl. Cover tightly with plastic wrap and let stand for 1 hour at room temperature before using.

Adapted from Ikaria: Lessons on Food, Life, and Longevity from the Greek Island Where People Forget to Die *(Rodale, 2014)*

Summer Greens Pie with Zucchini & Herbs

Χορτόπιτα καλοκαιρινή · *Hortopita kalokerini*

Ingredients *(Serves 8 to 10)*

- 3 pounds/1.5 kg zucchini, preferably large, coarsely grated
- Salt and freshly ground black pepper
- ½ cup/120 ml olive oil, plus ½ cup/120 ml for brushing the dough
- 3 large red onions, peeled and finely chopped
- 1 large fennel bulb, stalks removed, bulb finely chopped
- 8 oz/225 g amaranth leaves or Swiss chard, chopped
- 6 oz/170 g Greek feta, crumbled (1½ cups)
- 1 cup/60 g chopped fresh dill
- 1 cup/60 g chopped fresh mint
- 1 cup/60 g chopped fresh parsley
- 1 bunch finely chopped fresh oregano
- 5–10 squash blossoms, cleaned and finely chopped (optional)
- 1 recipe Basic Homemade Phyllo Dough, at room temperature (see p. 75)

1 Place the zucchini in a colander and toss with 1 tablespoon of salt. Set a plate on the zucchini and a weight, such as cans, on the plate. Let the zucchini drain for 1 to 3 hours, or overnight. Squeeze bunches of it at a time with your hands to wring out as much liquid as possible. Place in a large mixing bowl.

2 Preheat the oven to 375°F/190°C. Lightly oil a 15-inch/38-cm round baking or paella pan or a shallow, rectangular roasting pan (16 by 12 inches/40 by 30 cm).

3 Heat 2 tablespoons of the oil in a large frying pan over medium heat, add the onions and chopped fennel, and cook until soft. Add the amaranth. As soon as it wilts, remove the pan from the heat and let cool. Transfer the vegetables to the mixing bowl with the zucchini and add the feta, dill, mint, parsley, oregano, squash blossoms (if using), and the remaining 6 tablespoons of oil. Stir to blend and season with salt and pepper to taste.

4 Divide the dough into 4 balls. On a lightly floured surface, roll out the first dough ball, using the shape of your pan as the guide. For round pans, roll out to a circle about 18 inches/46 cm in diameter; for rectangular pans roll out to a rectangle about 3 inches/7.5 cm larger than the perimeter of the pan. Place the dough in the pan, leaving about 2 inches/5 cm hanging over the edge.

Brush with 2 tablespoons of the oil. Repeat with the second piece of dough. Brush that, too, with 2 tablespoons of the oil. Spread the filling evenly over the second layer of phyllo. Roll out the third piece of dough, place it over the filling, and press down gently. Brush with 2 tablespons of the oil. Roll out the last piece of dough to a slightly smaller diameter and place it over the surface of the pie. Join and fold in the bottom and top overhanging dough, rolling it decoratively around the perimeter of the pan to form a pretty rim. Brush the top of the pie with the remaining 2 tablespoons oil. Score into serving pieces.

Bake until the pastry is golden and crisp and the pie pulls away from the perimeter of the pan, 40 to 50 minutes. Let the pie cool slightly in the pan, and then serve.

If you're lucky enough to have access to wild fennel, use 2 cups, finely chopped, in place of the fennel bulb, and omit the dill. *i*

Adapted from Ikaria: Lessons on Food, Life, and Longevity from the Greek Island Where People Forget to Die *(Rodale, 2014)*

Leeks Cooked in Olive Oil with Tomatoes & Prunes

Πράσα λαδερά με ντομάτες και δαμάσκηνα
Prasa ladera me domates kai damaskina

1 Heat the oil in a large, wide pot or Dutch oven over medium heat. Add the onion, stir, reduce the heat to low, cover, and cook until very soft but not browned, about 10 minutes. Add the leeks and cook over low heat, covered, until al dente, about 12 minutes. Sprinkle in the flour and stir for a few minutes. Add the tomatoes to the pot and pour in the wine. Add the prunes and oregano sprigs. Season with salt and pepper to taste.

2 Cook the vegetables, partially covered, until the leeks are tender and the sauce is thick. If necessary, add a little water to the pot during cooking. Transfer the vegetables to a platter, sprinkle with paprika, and serve.

Adapted from The Country Cooking of Greece *(Chronicle Books, 2012)*

Ingredients *(Serves 4 as a vegetarian main course or 6 to 8 as a side dish)*

* ½ cup/120 ml extra-virgin Greek olive oil
* 1 large red onion, finely chopped or grated
* 2 pounds/910 g leeks, cut into 2-in/5-cm lengths, washed well, and drained
* 1 tbsp all-purpose flour
* 1 cup/240 ml peeled, seeded, and coarsely chopped plum tomatoes (canned are fine)
* ½ cup/120 ml white wine
* 10 pitted prunes
* 2–3 sprigs fresh oregano
* Salt and freshly ground black pepper
* Paprika

DIANE VON FURSTENBERG

Diane von Furstenberg first entered the fashion world in 1970 with a suitcase full of jersey dresses. Four years later, she created the wrap dress, which came to symbolize power and independence for an entire generation of women. By 1976, she had sold over a million of the dresses and was featured on the cover of Newsweek. *After relaunching in 1997 with the dress that started it all, DVF is now a global luxury lifestyle brand sold in over 55 countries. In 2005, Diane received the Lifetime Achievement Award from the Council of Fashion Designers of America (CFDA) for her impact on fashion, and one year later she was elected the CFDA's president. In 2015 Diane was named chairman of the organization. She also serves on the board of Culture Shed, a new center for artistic and cultural innovation in New York City, and the Statue of Liberty-Ellis Island Foundation. In 2014, Diane published a memoir,* The Woman I Wanted to Be, *and in 2015 she was named one of* Time *magazine's 100 Most Influential People. Diane is married to Barry Diller. She has two children, Alexander and Tatiana, and four grandchildren. With all of her successes, Diane happily maintains, "Children are my greatest creation."*

WHAT IS YOUR FAVORITE GREEK FOOD?

I love Greek food! All the elements that make up Greek food are wonderful, from the olives to the seafood to the honey. Lamb is by far my favorite meat. I love it when it's slow-roasted with Greek flavors—lemon, oregano, garlic, olives, bay—and served with fresh tzatziki and some warm flatbreads. Cruising around the Greek Islands means that the fishermen come to you, and they often have fresh octopus. I love it slow-cooked so that it is tender and juicy, and then grilled quickly to give it a char and some smoky flavor. Finish that with some lemon, and it's perfect. I love tomatoes in the summer, and Greece provides the perfect summer tomato that tastes like the sun. A quick tomato salad with Greek olives, fresh oregano, olive oil, red wine vinegar, and seasoning is a wonderful, simple dish.

IN A FEW WORDS, WHAT DOES GREECE MEAN TO YOU?

Greece to me is the crib of civilization. The most extraordinary place on earth.

WHAT IS YOUR FONDEST MEMORY OF GREECE?

Of course I love the islands . . . the sky . . . the earth. I have always loved mythology so I feel the presence of the gods when I'm there.

Roast Lamb with Garlic & Lemony Potatoes

Αρνί φούρνου σκορδάτο με λεμονάτες πατάτες
Arni fournou skordato me lemonates patates

Use any kind of broth you like in this recipe.
Be sure to remove the green shoots from the garlic cloves, as they can taste bitter.

1 Place the lamb in a roasting pan or clay baking dish with a lid. In a small bowl, mix the oil, garlic, 1 tablespoon of the mustard, and the rosemary and spread it over the lamb. Cover and let marinate at room temperature for at least 1 hour.

2 Preheat the oven to 325°F/160°C.

3 Sprinkle the potatoes with salt and pepper to taste and arrange them in the pan around the meat. Whisk the water with the remaining tablespoon of mustard and pour over the lamb and potatoes. Add the bay leaves, cover the pan (use aluminum foil if it doesn't have a lid), and roast for about 2 hours. Uncover the meat, sprinkle with lemon juice, raise the heat to 425°F/220°C and roast for another 30 minutes or so, until both meat and potatoes are nicely browned.

Ingredients *(Serves 6)*

- 1 (4 ½-lb/2-kg) lamb shoulder or leg, washed, dried, and trimmed
- ½ cup/120 ml olive oil
- 4 garlic cloves, coarsely chopped
- 2 tbsp mustard
- 1 tbsp chopped fresh rosemary, thyme, or oregano (or 1 tsp dried)
- 4 lb/2 kg potatoes, peeled and cut into uniform chunks
- Salt and freshly ground black pepper
- 3 cups/720 ml water or broth
- 2 bay leaves
- Juice of 2 lemons

Grilled Octopus

Χταπόδι στη σχάρα · Htapodi sti schara

Either a fresh octopus or a frozen one will work in this recipe. If the octopus is frozen, it will already be cleaned and will actually be more tender than a fresh one.

Ingredients *(Serves 4 to 6)*

* 1 (2-lb/1-kg) octopus, fresh or frozen (thawed)
* 2 bay leaves
* 10 peppercorns
* ½ cup/120 ml vinegar (optional)
* Olive oil
* Grated zest and juice of 1 lemon
* Freshly ground black pepper
* Dried oregano

1 Rinse the octopus well. Using a sharp knife, cut the octopus just below the eyes to remove the hood. Squeeze or cut out the beak and the cartilage on the other side of the beak. Rinse the octopus again, drain it, and place it in a large saucepan. Add the bay leaves and peppercorns and, if desired, add the vinegar and 1 cup/240 ml water. Cover and cook over medium heat until softened, 30 to 35 minutes. (Alternatively, cook the octopus in its own juices, without the water and vinegar; it will emit quite a bit of liquid but do keep an eye on it and add water if necessary to prevent it from sticking.)

2 While the octopus is cooking, light a gas or charcoal grill to medium-hot. Remove the octopus tentacles from the head. To expand the grilling surface and help them to cook faster, cut gashes lengthwise in the tentacles. Brush each tentacle with olive oil, place them on the grill, and cook for 2 to 3 minutes on each side. Slice the tentacles very thinly, drizzle with a little oil and lemon juice, sprinkle with pepper and oregano, and serve.

HRH PRINCESS IRENE

Princess Irene was born in Cape Town, South Africa, in 1942. From childhood, she participated in social work, together with her brother, then Crown Prince Constantine (subsequently King Constantine of the Hellenes), and her sister, Queen Sofía of Spain, accompanying their parents, King Paul and Queen Frederica of the Hellenes. The Royal Family resided in Greece until December, 1967. Princess Irene studied philosophy; archaeology, under Theophano Arvanitopoulou; and music (piano) under Gina Bachauer and Nadia Boulanger. She specialized in the study of comparative religions, focusing on the Orthodox Greek Church Fathers and the Vedanta Philosophy contained in the Vedas of India, specifically Advaita, during her sojourn in Madras, under T.M.P. Mahadevan, Director of the Centre for Advanced Study in Philosophy at the University of Madras.

Since childhood, Princess Irene and her siblings were trained by their parents to be aware of their good fortune. They traveled all over Greece as children, and Irene always remembers being struck by the extreme poverty she saw, particularly in the northern region of Epirus. This has shaped who she is today; she has dedicated her life to helping others who are less fortunate. In 1986, she founded the humanitarian organization World in Harmony, headquartered in Madrid, Spain. Its aim is to find practical ways of showing solidarity towards human beings in need and showing compassion to animals.

Princess Irene holds many honorary posts in various charitable organizations. She was instrumental to this project, as she is the one who introduced Tatiana to Boroume.

WHAT IS YOUR FAVORITE GREEK FOOD?

Greek food is fresh and tasty and, most importantly, served with love. For me, it is a blessing, as there is so much choice for us vegetarians. I can´t help thinking of the unimaginable number of Greeks and foreigners who are starving. I am praying that these people may soon find themselves enjoying a good meal. One of my favorite dishes is the simple yet delicious *fasolada* (bean soup), served piping hot with crusty bread in small local village tavernas. And the olive oil . . . on everything. And Greek coffee—one thing you cannot have abroad. I must say it is amusing to watch foreigners try and finish their Greek coffee! I love to enjoy it with a spoonful of *visino glyko* (sour cherry preserves). There is a Greek word for this enjoyment: *remvasmos*—literally translated as a break to enjoy your coffee, sit and contemplate . . . .

IN A FEW WORDS, WHAT DOES GREECE MEAN TO YOU?

Everything. Especially after having been away for so long.

WHAT IS YOUR FONDEST MEMORY OF GREECE?

I have so many. Now that I come back to Greece regularly, I notice how inspiring I find daily life here—what people find normal, I see as exciting.

One of my fondest memories is going in a Jeep with my parents, my sister, and my brother all over Greece while our parents were following up their projects in order to alleviate and encourage our compatriots. Intense love could be felt on both sides.

Bean Soup

Φασολάδα · Fasolada

Bean soup rivals moussaka (see p. 196) as the emblematic Greek national dish. There are countless small variations in recipes, with some cooks adding a chile pepper, others fragrant greens, still others a strip of dried orange peel. Some cooks also discard the water from the first boiling, in an attempt to reduce their "tooting" potential. Others do not add the salt, olive oil, and chopped tomatoes until the skins on a spoonful of beans puff up when blown on, in the belief that this trio slows down the cooking, making it practically impossible for the beans to soften.

1 Place the soaked beans in a large saucepan and cover with cold water. Bring to a boil and then drain. Rinse the saucepan, replace the beans, and add the carrots, celery, onions, parsley, and fresh water to cover. Bring to a boil and simmer until the beans are just tender (you can try blowing on them; if the skins peel back, they are ready). Add the tomatoes and oil and boil vigorously for 10 to 15 minutes. Season with salt and pepper to taste, and serve.

Ingredients *(Serves 6)*

* 1 lb/500 g dried navy beans, soaked overnight and drained
* 2–3 carrots, peeled and diced
* 2–3 celery stalks, thinly sliced
* 1 large or 2 medium onions, chopped
* 2 tbsp chopped fresh parsley
* 1 (28 oz/800 g) can chopped tomatoes, or 2 smaller cans
* ½ cup/120 ml olive oil
* Salt and freshly ground black pepper

Morello Cherry Spoon Sweet

Γλυκό του κουταλιού βύσσινο · Glyko tou koutaliou vissino

Spoon sweets are a cherished custom in Greece. They can be made with almost any kind of fruit and even some vegetables, like baby eggplant or tomatoes; nuts, like fresh walnuts or pistachios; and even lemon blossoms or rose petals. They resemble Western jams but are sweeter and more syrupy and are traditionally savored on their own, not spread on toast. They used to be a standard offering to any guest, expected or not, served on a small plate with a teaspoon and a glass of cold water. The more distinguished visitors also received a tiny cup of thick Greek coffee and possibly a liqueur as well. Nowadays, spoon sweets often appear at the end of a taverna meal on top of a plate of creamy yogurt. Quince, grape, and Morello cherry are among the most popular. They are also excellent on ice cream.

Ingredients *(Makes about 1 quart)*

- 2½ lb/1.2 kg Morello cherries, pitted, pits reserved
- 7½ cups/1.5 kg sugar
- 3-4 tbsp lemon juice

1. Place the cherry pits in a small saucepan, add 2 cups of water, bring to a boil, and simmer for 20 minutes. Put the pitted cherries and the sugar in a large saucepan in layers, first cherries, then sugar, cherries again, and so forth. Add ½ cup/120 ml of the strained "broth" from the boiled pits and any juices, and boil gently for about 25 minutes. Skim off the foam as it comes up. Remove from the heat and let stand for 12 hours, or overnight.

2. The next day, add the lemon juice and boil until you have a thick syrup. As you boil the cherries, boil 3 or 4 jam jars in a separate covered saucepan to sterilize them. When your sweet is ready, remove the jars from the water, turn them upside down to drain on paper towels, and then ladle the cherries and their syrup into them. Fill right up to the top, put on the lids, and then turn upside down again and leave to cool. This will create a vacuum and prevent the sweet from going moldy. Store in a dark place.

JIM GIANOPULOS

James N. Gianopulos is the chairman and CEO of 20th Century Fox, *overseeing the motion picture divisions of Twentieth Century Fox Film Corp., which include Fox 2000, Fox Searchlight Pictures, Fox Animation Studios, Blue Sky Studios, Fox International Productions, and their related entities. One of the longest-tenured studio chairmen in the film industry, Mr. Gianopulos has been involved in the evolution of new entertainment media and technologies for more than 25 years, and is considered a leading strategist in the industry.*

During his 16-year tenure at Fox, he has overseen a broad range of successful films, most recently including Deadpool, The Martian, The Revenant, Kingsman: The Secret Service, Birdman, 12 Years a Slave, X-Men: Days of Future Past, Life of Pi, Dawn of the Planet of the Apes, The Fault in Our Stars, The Grand Budapest Hotel, *and the two highest-grossing films of all time,* Avatar *and* Titanic, *among many others. Prior to his current post, Mr. Gianopulos was chairman and CEO of Fox Filmed Entertainment, and before that, he was president of* 20th Century Fox *International, a position he had held since 1994. Before joining* 20th Century Fox, *Mr. Gianopulos held senior management positions at Paramount and Columbia Pictures.*

WHAT IS YOUR FAVORITE GREEK FOOD?

Real Greek yogurt, not the brand names that have now proliferated, but the real stuff. My grandfather used to make it in our house in New York in the basement. He would borrow all the pots and blankets he could find, disappear for a while, and he would have his home laboratory in the basement. I never really understood the process but the result was amazing, and nothing I've tasted since has been as authentic.

IN A FEW WORDS, WHAT DOES GREECE MEAN TO YOU?
Greece is a spirit, a way of thinking, of living, of accepting all of the joys and challenges of existence and making the most of all of them. It's also the most beautiful place in the world.

WHAT IS YOUR FONDEST MEMORY OF GREECE?
That's like asking my favorite film—it's impossible, and a new one happens every summer, but I can always see the color of the sea in my mind when I'm away, and it serves to quell the yearning until the next time.

While it is hard to pick just a few of the many wonderful dishes of Greece, here are the first that come to mind. I eat mostly vegetables and fish, and Greek cuisine affords plenty of options. These are among my favorites, mostly for nostalgic reasons and memories of my family.

Garlic Sauce

Σκορδαλιά · Skordalia

My mother made the most amazing skordalia, *and growing up I remember eating it with various vegetables or just a great loaf of bread. It also goes well with fried zucchini and eggplant. But the cool, sweet taste of boiled beets combined with the tart and bold taste of garlic was always my favorite.*

Ingredients *(Serves 6)*

* 2 slices rustic bread, crusts removed
* 5–6 garlic cloves
* Sea salt
* 1 cup/145 g walnuts or blanched almonds
* About 1 cup/240 ml extra-virgin olive oil
* ¼ cup/60 ml vinegar or 3 tbsp lemon juice

I Soak the bread in water and squeeze it dry. Pound the garlic in a mortar with some salt until you have a smooth paste. Grind the nuts in a food processor, add the bread, and process to blend. With the processor on, dribble in the oil and vinegar until you have a nice, creamy sauce. If using lemon juice, add it slowly at the end. If the *skordalia* seems too thick, add a tablespoon or so of cold water.

i *Ground blanched almonds will make a white* skordalia. *Walnuts turn it darker but they taste even more delicious. You may find yourself eating this by the spoonful on its own. Or use it like an aioli with Fisherman's Soup* *(see p. 92).*

Fisherman's Soup

Κακαβιά · Kakavia

I've always loved kakavia, *which my father told me he enjoyed in his youth as an engineer on ships. It is also easy to make, and at some point I was told that the best ingredient was a few tablespoons of the Aegean, which I always thought gave it a special flavor, or at least was a very fitting way to add some salt and the love of the sea at the same time. Serve with toasted bread or Cretan rusks spread with a little* skordalia *for a Gallic touch.*

Ingredients *(Serves 6)*

* 1 lb/500 g potatoes, peeled and quartered
* 2 onions, quartered
* 2 carrots, peeled and sliced
* 3–4 celery stalks, sliced
* 3–4 sprigs parsley
* 2 bay leaves
* ⅓ cup/80 ml olive oil
* Salt and freshly ground pepper
* 2 lb/1 kg rockfish, red snapper, or sea bass, cleaned, scaled, and gutted, head reserved
* 1–2 lb/500 g–1 kg scrubbed mussels and/or clams, peeled shrimp, or whatever mixed shellfish are available
* 3–4 tablespoons lemon juice

1 Put the potatoes, onions, carrots, celery, parsley, and bay leaves in a large pot or Dutch oven. Add the oil, season with salt and pepper, and pour in enough water to cover and then some. Boil furiously until the vegetables are barely tender. Strain, reserving the liquid, and set the potatoes, celery, and carrots aside. When cool enough to handle, cut the vegetables in small pieces.

2 Pour the liquid back into the pot and add the fish (including the head, which has so much flavor and gelatin). The liquid should reach about three-quarters of the way up the fish; add a little water if necessary. Boil rapidly until the flesh near the bones is no longer pink, about 15 minutes. Lift out the fish, remove the bones and fins, and cut into chunks. Strain the broth and return it to the pot along with the fish, vegetables, shellfish, and lemon juice. Bring back to a boil and simmer until the shellfish open. Serve.

i *Editors' note:* Kakavia *is named after the pot (*kakavi*) fishermen used to cook it in and, as with the French bouillabaisse, there's a lot of discussion about what fish must be used to make it. A true* kakavia *contains whatever the catch of the day was, boiled with only onion and potatoes and a dash of the Aegean, but this version is a bit more sophisticated, with a good stock, more vegetables, and some shellfish added at the end. It also calls for a large amount of olive oil to make the soup extremely rich and smooth, but if you wish to reduce the amount, do so and it will still be good. Fast boiling is another prerequisite for blending the oil and water into a velouté.*

Oven-Baked Greek-Style Ratatouille

Μπριάμ · Briam

My grandmother came from Constantinople, and used to make a wonderful baked vegetable dish she called tourlou, *I assume the Turkish name for it, which means "all mixed up," and which I later learned was called* briam *when I went to find a recipe. It does not challenge my culinary skills so I make it often, and it makes a great side dish or, with some brown rice, a full meal on its own. I love making it in Greece in the summer, when the tomatoes and zucchini and all the many vegetables and herbs are at their freshest and most fragrant.*

1 Preheat the oven to 375°F/190°C.

2 Put all the vegetables and seasonings in a large roasting pan and toss them in the oil so that they are all coated. Add a little water, about ¼ cup/60 ml, and bake until all the vegetables are tender, 1½ to 2 hours. Check from time to time and add more water if they start to stick.

i *Editors' note: This dish is good hot and at room temperature. Like so many dishes cooked with olive oil, it's delicious the next day, too. If you happen to have any* halloumi *cheese on hand, it makes an interesting addition to both the taste and the texture.*

Ingredients *(Serves 8)*

- 2 lb/1 kg zucchini, cut into ½-in/12-mm slices
- 2 lb/1 kg eggplant, cut into ½-in/12-mm slices
- 6–8 tomatoes, peeled and coarsely chopped
- 3 potatoes, cut into ½-in/12-mm slices
- 3 green bell peppers, seeded and diced
- 3 red onions, sliced
- ½ cup/30 g chopped fresh parsley
- Handful fresh basil leaves, torn
- 3 garlic cloves, finely chopped, or to taste
- 1 tsp dried oregano
- Salt and freshly ground black pepper
- ½ cup/120 ml olive oil, more is even better

JIM STOTT & JONATHAN KING

Jim Stott and Jonathan King are the founders of Stonewall Kitchen in Maine. The two share a passion for gardening and food. In 1991, after encouragement from friends who had tasted their homemade jams and condiments, they set up shop at a local farmers' market. To their surprise, everything sold. Each Saturday they would return, usually with some new item added to the offering. One Saturday, a local merchant bought out the whole stand so that she could stock her shelves with the products, which were not only delicious but beautiful as well. Today Stonewall Kitchen products can be found in thousands of stores across the United States and in 43 other countries. They have won more awards than any other food company in the United States. The same guiding principle that the pair started with can be found in each of their products today: Start with the best ingredients you can find, treat them with care, and wholesome deliciousness will be the reward.

WHAT IS YOUR FAVORITE GREEK FOOD?

All the foods we tasted in Greece were not only fresh and delicious but seemed to ooze with the traditions and dreams of the people who cooked them. They screamed "celebrate life!" We too love to celebrate life with food and friends but have found that easy and casual is the way we prefer to do it. Who wants to be stuck in the kitchen while all your friends are laughing and enjoying each other's company?

IN A FEW WORDS, WHAT DOES GREECE MEAN TO YOU?

When we think of Greece we immediately think of food, celebration, and family. To us, the three are inseparable.

WHAT IS YOUR FONDEST MEMORY OF GREECE?

Visiting the city of Athens and the beautiful sundrenched islands.

Spanakopita Re-Do

Σπανακόπιτα «αλλιώς» · Spanakopita "allios"

Spanakopita, *aka spinach pie, is a Greek classic, and so delicious. Creamy, satisfying cheese mixed with warm garlic-scented spinach; what could be better? Add a cocktail, some friends . . . pure magic! We've found a way to update this classic into an easy-to-pass-around, one-handed bite.*

1 Preheat the oven to 325°F/170°F.

2 Heat the oil in a large skillet over medium heat. Add the garlic and cook, stirring, for 30 seconds. Add the spinach in handfuls and stir to cook it down, about 4 minutes. Remove from the heat and finely chop the spinach. Return the spinach to the skillet over medium heat. Add the cream, nutmeg, and salt and pepper to taste; cook until the cream thickens slightly, about 4 minutes. Remove from the heat, add half the feta and taste for seasoning, adding more salt and pepper or nutmeg as needed.

3 Place the phyllo cups on a baking sheet. Divide the spinach mixture between the cups and top each one with some of the remaining feta. Bake until the cheese has melted and the spinach mixture is hot and bubbling, about 10 minutes. Serve hot or at room temperature.

i *The cups can be assembled up to 2 months ahead of time; cover tightly with foil and plastic wrap and freeze. Increase the baking time to 12 to 15 minutes.*

Ingredients

(Serves 12)

* 1½ tbsp olive oil
* 2 garlic cloves, minced
* 6 oz/170 g baby spinach
* ⅓ cup/75 ml heavy cream
* ⅛ tsp ground nutmeg
* Salt and freshly ground black pepper
* 2 oz/55 g feta cheese, finely crumbled (½ cup)
* 12 mini phyllo pastry cups.

Lamb & Feta Sliders

Αρνίσια μπιφτεκάκια με φέτα • Arnisia biftekakia me feta

Is it a meatball or a slider? Call it what you like, but enjoy the rich flavor of ground lamb mixed with caramelized onions, earthy rosemary, creamy feta cheese, and crunchy panko breadcrumbs. Make the sliders ahead of time if you're serving a crowd and simply reheat them in a 300°F/150°C oven until hot, 5 to 10 minutes. If you want to serve these as meatballs, don't flatten them before cooking, and omit the pita bread and toppings.

Ingredients

(Makes 18 meatballs or sliders)

- 3 tbsp olive oil
- 1 small onion, finely chopped
- 1 garlic clove, finely chopped
- 2½ tbsp chopped fresh rosemary
- Salt and freshly ground black pepper
- 1 lb/ 500 kg ground lamb
- 1½ cups/75 g panko breadcrumbs
- 2 oz/55 g feta cheese, crumbled (½ cup)
- 1 large egg
- Pita breads
- Thick, chunky ketchup and/or 1 cup/280 g Greek yogurt mixed with 2 tbsp chopped fresh rosemary

1 Heat 1 tablespoon of the oil in a medium skillet over medium-low heat. Add the onion, 1 tablespoon of the rosemary, the garlic, and salt and pepper to taste and cook, stirring occasionally, for 10 minutes. Transfer to a large bowl and let cool slightly. Add the lamb, ½ cup/25 g of the panko, the feta, egg, and the remaining 1½ tablespoons rosemary to the onion mixture and season with salt and pepper. Mix well to combine and then roll the mixture into eighteen 2-inch/5-cm balls and flatten slightly to form into sliders.

2 Place the remaining panko in a bowl. Roll each slider lightly in the panko to coat on all sides. (The sliders can be made 1 day ahead up to this point; cover and refrigerate until ready to cook.)

3 Heat the remaining 2 tablespoons oil in a large skillet over medium-high heat. When the oil is hot (test it with a couple of the breadcrumbs; they should sizzle right away) add the sliders, making sure not to crowd the skillet. (You may need to make them in two batches.) Cook until they are golden brown and cooked through, about 4 minutes on each side. If the sliders start to burn or turn dark brown reduce the heat slightly. Cut one open to make sure there is no sign of pinkness. Serve hot on pita bread with a dollop of ketchup or yogurt on top.

LAURIE CONSTANTINO

Laurie Constantino is a food writer who also teaches cooking and foraging. She lives with her Greek American husband in Anchorage, Alaska and Limnos, Greece. Her cookbook Tastes Like Home: Mediterranean Cooking in Alaska *was published in 2007. Her next cookbook,* Greek Cooking in America: The Best Recipes from Greek Festivals and Community Cookbooks, *will contain recipes from four generations of Greek immigrant women and will document how traditional recipes changed and evolved in America. The recipes are curated and adapted from community cookbooks in Laurie's one-of-a-kind collection of 600 Greek and Greek American cookbooks.*

WHAT IS YOUR FAVORITE GREEK FOOD?

Sea urchin roe directly from the Aegean Sea, with a tiny squeeze of lemon, and scooped up with a chunk of rustic bread. If I could choose, this would be my last meal on earth.

IN A FEW WORDS, WHAT DOES GREECE MEAN TO YOU?

Greek friends and family have taught me to find joy in life's ordinary events, to share the best of what I have with others, and to remember that humanity's most important task is to give and receive love.

WHAT IS YOUR FONDEST MEMORY OF GREECE?

The sun is shining and streets are still. I'm with loved ones in a shady seaside taverna, sated on grilled sardines, sun-ripened tomatoes, and crispy fried zucchini. We throw bits of leftover bread into the sparkling sea and laugh at little fish swirling, twirling, and racing for the bread.

Pastitsio with Greens

Παστίτσιο με χόρτα · Pastitsio me horta

Pastitsio with greens is a splendid vegetarian alternative to pastitsio with meat sauce, a traditional dish some call "Greek lasagna." Abundant greens and fresh herbs balance the three cheeses used in this recipe. Any wild or domesticated greens may be used, but for better flavor, use at least two or more different varieties. I've made this with various combinations of spinach, chard, Tuscan kale, endive, nettles, lamb's quarters, dandelions, vlita *(amaranth greens), and other edible greens. This pastitsio may be assembled up to 24 hours ahead and baked just before serving, making it a great dish for entertaining. Because made-ahead, refrigerated pastitsio goes into the oven cold, it takes at least 10 minutes longer to bake.*

1 Preheat the oven to 350°F/180°C.

2 Bring a large pot of salted water to a boil. Add the pasta and cook until it's almost, but not quite, done. Remove the pasta with a slotted spoon to a bowl of ice water; reserve the pasta water for blanching the greens. Drain the pasta and set aside.

3 *For the filling:* Return the pasta-cooking water to a boil and blanch the greens for 1 minute, then transfer to a bowl of ice water. Using your hands, squeeze as much water as possible from the greens. Chop the greens and put them in a large mixing bowl. Heat the oil in a large skillet over medium heat. Add the onions, season with salt and pepper, and cook, stirring, until they soften and start to turn golden. Stir in the garlic and Aleppo pepper (if using) and cook for 1 minute. Add the cooked onions, green onions, parsley, dill, mint, feta, *kasseri*, and *manouri* to the bowl with the greens. Toss well to combine thoroughly. Season with salt and pepper to taste.

Ingredients *(Serves 6 to 9)*

* 8 oz/225 g miniature penne or other hollow pasta

Filling

* 1 lb/455 g spinach or other wild or domesticated greens, washed and trimmed
* 1 lb/455 g Swiss chard or other wild or domesticated greens, washed and trimmed
* 2 tbsp olive oil
* 2 cups/320 g chopped yellow onions
* Salt and freshly ground black pepper
* 1 tbsp minced garlic
* 1 tsp Aleppo pepper or ½ tsp red pepper flakes (optional)
* 1 cup/100 g thinly sliced green onions
* ½ cup/30 g minced fresh parsley
* ¼ cup/15 g minced fresh dill
* ¼ cup/15 g minced fresh mint
* 3 oz/85 g feta cheese, crumbled (¾ cup)
* 6 oz/170 g *kasseri* or *graviera* cheese, grated (may substitute *fontina*)
* 6 oz/170 g fresh *manouri* or *anthotyro* cheese, crumbled (may substitute ricotta)

4 *For the béchamel:* Warm the milk gently on the stovetop or in the microwave; remove it from the heat just before it boils. Melt the butter in a large saucepan, whisk in the flour to make a smooth paste, and cook for 2 minutes, stirring constantly. Slowly whisk in the warm milk and cook, stirring, until the sauce is smooth and is the thickness of heavy cream. Add the nutmeg and salt and pepper to taste. Pour ½ cup of the hot milk sauce into the pasta and stir to evenly distribute. Put the egg yolks in a small bowl and quickly whisk in ½ cup of the hot milk sauce, then return the mixture to the saucepan. Cook over very low heat for 2 minutes, stirring constantly; be careful not to let the sauce get hotter than a low simmer. Remove from the heat.

5 *For the topping:* Mix the *kefalotyri* with the panko.

6 To assemble, place half the pasta in a well-oiled 10-inch/25-cm square baking pan. Spread half the filling over the pasta. Top with the remaining pasta, and then with the remaining filling. Spread the béchamel over the final layer of filling. Sprinkle the breadcrumb topping over the béchamel. Bake until the top of the pastitsio is golden and its juices are bubbling, 35 to 40 minutes. Let cool for 15 to 30 minutes before cutting into rectangles and serving. (If you cut the pastitsio immediately after removing it from the oven, the layers will fall apart, but it will still taste great.)

Béchamel

* 2½ cups/600 ml whole milk
* 4 tbsp/55 g unsalted butter
* ¼ cup/35 g all-purpose flour
* ¼ tsp nutmeg
* Salt and freshly ground black pepper
* 2 egg yolks

Topping

* ⅓ cup freshly grated *kefalotyri* cheese (may substitute Parmesan)
* ⅓ cup/15 g panko breadcrumbs

Mushroom Stifado

Μανιτάρια στιφάδο · Manitaria stifado

Nature's seasons and religious fasting periods profoundly influence what Greek island villagers eat. Many are farmers, relying for sustenance on the fruits—and vegetables—of their labors. Most supplement their diets with wild greens and snails, mushrooms and sea urchins, rabbits and octopus. One year, the confluence of perfect rains and warm temperatures brought forth an unexpected bounty of wild mushrooms, gathered from a Limnian mountain pasture, just in time for the first day of Great Lent. After vetting their edibility with a knowledgeable aunt (the primary rule of mushroom foraging is "when in doubt, throw it out"), I made vegan, Lenten-friendly mushroom stew, modeled after stifado*, a classic Greek dish.*

Mushroom stifado *tastes best when made with wild mushrooms; my second choice is a mixture of cultivated cremini, oyster, and shiitake mushrooms. However, even when made with a single type of mushroom, this savory stew is a treat. Sautéing mushrooms in small batches is the key to releasing their full flavor; if you cook too many at one time, they'll release all their liquid and steam rather than brown. Because each vegetable is salted separately (salt helps them cook more evenly), be careful about how much salt you add at any one time or the finished dish may be too salty. Serve as an appetizer, over pasta tossed with garlic and olive oil, or on its own with roasted potatoes and a crisp green salad. Leftovers, chopped and mixed with stock, make a flavorful soup.*

1 Heat 2 tablespoons of the oil in a large skillet, add the pearl onions, and season with salt and pepper to taste.
Cook until the onions are well browned on all sides and cooked through. Using a slotted spoon, transfer the browned onions to a small bowl and set aside. Add one-third of the mushrooms to the empty pan, season with salt and pepper, and cook over medium-high heat until they're well browned on all sides. If the pan is too dry for the mushrooms to brown properly, add 1 to 2 tablespoons oil. Though you want the mushrooms to caramelize, be careful they don't burn; turn down the heat if necessary.

Ingredients *(Serves 4 to 6)*

* 2–8 tbsp/30–120 ml olive oil (may substitute any vegetable oil)
* 1 lb/455 g pearl onions, peeled, or 14 oz/400 g frozen pearl onions, thawed
* Salt and freshly ground black pepper
* 1½ lb/680 g mushrooms, cleaned, trimmed, and cut in 1-in/2.5 cm chunks
* 2 cups coarsely chopped onions
* 2 tbsp minced garlic
* 1 tsp Aleppo pepper or ½ tsp red pepper flakes (optional)

2 Transfer the mushrooms to a separate bowl and repeat with the remaining oil (as needed) and mushrooms, in two batches. Add the chopped onions to the pan, season lightly with salt and pepper, and cook until they soften and begin to turn golden, adding olive oil if necessary. As the onions cook, scrape up any browned bits from the bottom of the pan. Stir in the garlic and Aleppo pepper (if using) and cook for 1 minute.

Stir in the wine and cook until it's reduced by half. Stir in the tomatoes, vinegar, rosemary, and sugar. Bring to a boil, cover, reduce the heat to low, and simmer for 15 minutes. Stir in the mushrooms and simmer for 15 minutes. Stir in the pearl onions and simmer for 5 minutes. Serve immediately.

* 1 cup/240 ml red wine
* 1 (15-oz/430-g) can chopped tomatoes or 2 cups fresh, with juices
* 2 tbsp red wine vinegar
* 1 tbsp minced fresh rosemary
* 2 tsp sugar

Salmon Kleftiko

Σολωμός κλέφτικος · Solomos kleftikos

During the 19th-century Greek War of Independence against the Ottoman Turks, the Klefts were irregular guerrilla fighters. They famously stole Ottoman-owned sheep and cooked them underground to keep the cooking smell from giving away their location. Traditionally, Klefts cooked the meat in buried lambskins or clay pots. In modern versions of Kleft-style cooking, meat, vegetables, and seasonings are wrapped tightly in foil or parchment paper, and slowly cooked in the oven. The meat ends up succulent, with all its flavor sealed inside the packet.

Salmon Kleftiko uses the same closed-container technique. Unlike lamb, salmon cooks quickly, making this dish perfect for days when you're in a hurry. The packets go together quickly and bake for only 15 minutes. Inside, fish juices mingle with tomatoes to form a light, flavorful sauce. Cooked this way, the fish stays tender and juicy. Even better, there aren't any pots to clean. For making the packets, I prefer foil because it's easiest to use. Parchment paper makes a more attractive presentation and may be substituted for foil; if using parchment, be sure to seal the edges tightly. I'm usually too lazy to peel tomatoes; I do here because peeled tomatoes make a better sauce. This step, however, is optional. Don't forget to put an empty platter on the table as a place to discard the wrappings.

Ingredients *(Serves 6)*

* 12 small tomatoes or 24 cherry tomatoes
* 2 lb/1 kg skinless salmon fillet, cut into 6 even pieces
* Salt and freshly ground black pepper
* ¼ cup/60 ml olive oil
* 2–3 tsp dried oregano, crushed
* ¼ cup/40 g oil-cured black olives, pitted and chopped

1. Preheat the oven to 450°F/230°C.

2. To peel the tomatoes (optional), cut a shallow X in the bottom of each tomato and drop in boiling water for 30 seconds. Using a slotted spoon, transfer the tomatoes to a bowl of ice water and slip off their skins. Cut small tomatoes in ½-inch/12-mm-thick slices or cut cherry tomatoes in half.

3. Lightly season the salmon on both sides with salt and pepper. Oil six 18-inch/46-cm-long sheets of heavy-duty aluminum foil. Place 1 salmon fillet in the center of each foil piece. Sprinkle the salmon fillets with oregano and chopped olives. Top with the tomatoes and salt lightly. Drizzle with olive oil. Fold the foil over the salmon so the edges meet.

Seal the edges all the way around, making tight ½-inch/12-mm folds, then fold again to make a tight seal. Allow space on the sides for circulation and expansion. (The recipe may be made to this point, up to 4 hours ahead.)

4 Bake for 15 minutes. Place the packets on serving plates. Cut a large X across the top of each packet; fold back the foil to expose the fish, being careful of hot steam. Serve immediately.

MARGARET ATWOOD

Canadian writer Margaret Atwood is the author of more than 40 volumes of poetry, children's literature, fiction, and nonfiction, but she is best known for her novels, which include The Edible Woman, The Handmaid's Tale, The Robber Bride, Alias Grace, *and* The Blind Assassin, *which won the prestigious Booker Prize in 2000. Her latest work is a book of short stories called* Stone Mattress: Nine Tales *(2014). Her newest novel,* MaddAddam *(2013), is the final volume in a three-book series that began with the Man-Booker prize-nominated* Oryx and Crake *and continued with* The Year of the Flood. *Her most recent volume of poetry,* The Door, *was published in 2007.* In Other Worlds: SF and the Human Imagination, *a collection of nonfiction essays appeared in 2011. Her nonfiction book,* Payback: Debt and the Shadow Side of Wealth *was adapted for the screen in 2012. Ms. Atwood's work has been published in more than 40 languages, including Farsi, Japanese, Turkish, Finnish, Korean, Icelandic, Greek, and Estonian. Margaret Atwood lives in Toronto with writer Graeme Gibson.*

WHAT IS YOUR FAVORITE GREEK FOOD?

I am especially fond of Greek yogurt and Greek olives.

IN A FEW WORDS, WHAT DOES GREECE MEAN TO YOU?

I began reading Greek myths when I was still in grade school, and continued in high school with the *Iliad, the Odyssey*, and Robert Graves's guide to Greek mythology. I also read the *Aeneid*, as I was studying Latin. I went on to study English literature, and a knowledge of Greek mythology is essential for that—certainly anything before 1900.

So Greece is an epic place, and an imaginative homeland for anyone immersed in literature, as I have been. These stories have inspired many writers, as well as many plays and operas. They are a foundation stone of Western literature and culture.

WHAT IS YOUR FONDEST MEMORY OF GREECE?
We had a wonderful visit to Mycenae and another to Epidaurus, in the summer of 2014. These are astonishing places. Just as impressive was the knowledge of our drivers—one of them was able to describe the battle of Salamis as if it had happened yesterday. A little owl of Athena that I got in Athens sits on my desk as a reminder.

Vicky Vlachonis on Greek yogurt:
Organic Greek yogurt contains probiotics, which are essential for gut health. Look for yogurts with lactobacillus, streptococcus, and bifidobacteria. We have 100 trillion different bacteria in our bodies, up to two pounds/1 kg of which are lurking in our intestines. You probably know that these microbes impact your digestion and your immunity—but did you realize the balance of bacteria in your gut could impact your level of pain, both physically and emotionally? The microbes that live in your gut can either help keep you healthy and happy, or make you susceptible to conditions such as type 2 diabetes, obesity, inflammatory bowel disease, colon cancer, and autoimmune disorders such as rheumatoid arthritis. Every day, your healthy and unhealthy strains of bacteria are in a constant battle with each other for domination of your entire body, including your brain. Feelings of stress and emotional strain often "get us in the gut," for good reason: Similar to the spinal cord, we have about 100 billion neurons in the small intestine alone. Almost every known neurotransmitter (and their receptors) can be found in this "second brain." The gut, not the brain, is also the body's largest producer of serotonin, our primary happiness hormone. However, without enough healthy digestive bacteria, neither your gut nor your brain can properly produce enough serotonin for regular bowel and brain functions, which is why changing the balance of the bacteria in your gut can significantly impact the amount of pain you feel, both physically and emotionally. This is why it's good to eat 6 ounces of yogurt every day.

Yogurt Soufflé

Σουφλέ με γιαούρτι · Soufle me yiaourti

Thick, creamy Greek yogurt and thyme-scented honey are among the country's trademark tastes. Delectable at any time, yogurt may be served for breakfast in hotels and for dessert in many tavernas, offered free and if not with honey, then with their own spoon sweets made of sour cherries, orange, grape, or quince. But for a special dinner, try this soufflé and pair it with your own jams, with fresh fruit like raspberries or strawberries, or with stewed fruit like apricots or peaches.

1 Preheat the oven to 350°F/180°C. Grease an 8-inch/21-cm soufflé dish with the butter and dust with sugar to prevent sticking.

2 Beat the egg yolks with the sugar in a bowl until pale and stir in the yogurt and cornstarch gradually. In a separate bowl, beat the egg whites until they form stiff peaks and fold them gently into the mixture. Pour into the prepared soufflé dish.

3 Set a pan of hot water in the oven, set the soufflé dish in the pan, and bake until the soufflé puffs right up and turns golden, about 25 minutes. Serve.

Ingredients *(Serves 6)*

* 1 tbsp unsalted butter
* 1 cup/200 g sugar, plus extra for the soufflé dish
* 3 eggs, separated, plus 2 egg whites
* 1¼ cups/275 g Greek yogurt
* 2 tbsp cornstarch

MARY KATRANTZOU

Mary Katrantzou was born in Athens in 1983, to an interior designer mother and a father who worked in textile design. Having developed an appreciation of applied design from an early age, she moved to America to study architecture at the Rhode Island School of Design, before transferring to Central Saint Martins in London to complete her B.A. degree in textile design. Mary next shifted her focus to womenswear, with an emphasis on print. She became interested in the way that printed textiles can change the shape of a woman's body and went on to graduate with an M.A. in Fashion from Central Saint Martins with distinction. Her first ready-to-wear collection debuted at London Fashion Week in spring/summer 2009. Small but impressive, it picked up 15 stockists, a number which now stands at 230 of the most prestigious stores. Mary's collections have been based thematically on perfume bottles, interiors and objects of art, flower fields, everyday objects, vintage postage stamps, landscapes, and, most recently, shoes, all keeping the printed image central to her aesthetic. Her latest shows feature symbols expressing the concept of movement, of voyage into uncharted territories.

WHAT IS YOUR FAVORITE GREEK FOOD?

Yemista, which are stuffed tomatoes and peppers cooked in the oven with rice, ground meat, raisins, pine nuts, tomato juice, fresh onions, fresh parsley and dill. They are perfect for Sunday lunch with the family. Pastitsio (see pp. 102, 129), or baked macaroni casserole, reminds me of my grandmother, as she used to cook it for me all the time when I was younger and spent time with her in Eretria (Evia). *Dakos*—Cretan barley rusk (dried bread) topped with chopped tomatoes, feta or *myzithra* cheese, capers, oregano, and delicious olive oil. Best consumed on a beautiful Greek island, at a taverna by the sea.

IN A FEW WORDS, WHAT DOES GREECE MEAN TO YOU?

It's home, it's part of me, it's love, it's where I feel free. When I go back, I always feel like I never left. There is an innocence and a purity that I relate to my years growing up in Greece. Every time I touch down in Athens I feel at peace.

WHAT IS YOUR FONDEST MEMORY OF GREECE?

The magical hour of the sunset falling over the island of Spetses. We have a summer house there and I go every year, so it brings back a lot of memories. The smell of bougainvillea and the sea breeze are instilled in me forever.

Stuffed Tomatoes & Peppers

Γεμιστά · Yemista

These tomatoes and peppers are excellent served at room temperature and, like so many other dishes cooked with olive oil, are even better the next day.

1 Preheat the oven to 375°F/190°C.

2 Slice the caps off the tomatoes and scoop out the insides into a bowl, being careful not to pierce the skin. Take the tops off the peppers and remove the core and seeds. Save all the vegetable caps near their mates for replacement later. Sprinkle the cavities of the tomatoes with a tiny pinch of salt and sugar.

3 *For the filling:* Heat 2 tablespoons of the oil in a large skillet over medium heat and cook the onions and garlic until translucent. Add the ground beef and cook until it's no longer pink. Add half the grated tomatoes, the parsley, mint, rice, pine nuts, currants, tomato paste–water mixture, and salt and pepper to taste and cook, stirring, until the rice has absorbed most of the liquid. Set aside and let cool a bit.

Ingredients *(Serves 6)*

* 6 large, firm tomatoes
* 6 green bell peppers
* Salt
* Sugar

Filling

* ¼ cup/60 ml olive oil
* 1–2 large onions, coarsely chopped
* 2–3 garlic cloves, coarsely chopped
* 8 oz/250 g ground beef
* 2 lb/1kg ripe tomatoes, halved, seeded and grated, skins discarded
* 1 small bunch parsley, finely chopped
* ½ cup/30 g chopped fresh mint
* ½ cup/100 g short-grain rice
* 5 tbsp/40 g pine nuts
* 5 tbsp/45 g currants
* 1 tbsp tomato paste dissolved in ¼ cup/60 ml water (optional)
* Salt and freshly ground black pepper
* 1 cup/240 ml vegetable broth or water

4 Stuff each vegetable with the mixture until it is about ¾ full (overstuffing may burst them), and put back their caps. Place the stuffed tomatoes and peppers in a large baking pan. Drizzle the remaining 2 tablespoons oil and remaining grated tomatoes over them, pour in the broth, and bake for about 1 hour. Serve.

i *Needless to say, there are hundreds of variations on this theme—you can use any herbs you like; substitute hard, piquant cheese for the meat; omit the meat altogether and add more rice (2 cups/400 g, instead of ½ cup/50 g); and so forth. Stick wedges of potato between the peppers and tomatoes for an extra treat.*

MICHEL ROUX

Michel Roux is a French-born chef and restaurateur who has been working in the UK since the mid-60s. Together with his brother Albert, he opened Le Gavroche in London, which was later to become the first restaurant in Britain to earn three Michelin stars, and The Waterside Inn, which was the first restaurant outside France to hold three stars for as long as 25 years.
Like his brother, Michel began as a pastry chef, although he almost pursued a career as an opera singer. After his military service, he joined Albert in London, though he didn't speak a word of the language. In time, the enormous success of their restaurants has led them to be called the "godfathers of modern restaurant cuisine in the UK."
Michel has received two lifetime achievement awards and is a member of several orders in France, including the National Order of Merit and the Legion of Honor. In 2004 he was made an honorary Officer of the British Empire. Besides founding the Roux Brothers Scholarship with Albert in 1984, he has worked as a consultant for such companies as British Airways and Celebrity Cruises and has trained an impressive number of today's top chefs.

WHAT IS YOUR FAVORITE GREEK FOOD?

Quite simply, Greek food is fiercely local and exquisitely simple but always fresh, unpretentious and evocative of the colors, scents, and flavors of the landscape, a place to spend languorous hours sharing meals with friends and family. Here, the *meze* feast is not only a glorious necessity, it seems to epitomize the whole of Greece in its pungent variety—the wide blue skies and sea, the moonlight, the warmth of its people, the wisdom of its philosophers, and its infinite, bewitching history. A favorite little dish is octopus with smooth *fava* (see p. 156), creamy split yellow peas served with lemon and fresh oregano.

In Greece I have sampled the most stunning seafood, including deliciously perfect calamari served in a simple taverna in Kefalonia in the shadow of a 16th-century fortress next to a little bay. I've had sublime lamb on the bone with nothing more than rice pilaf allowed to cook in the lamb juices, served with village yogurt—a rustic dish I enjoy when visiting friends on the island of Samos. And one of my fondest food memories is swimming out to some rocks on a boat trip, grabbing sea urchins, breaking, and eating them on the spot, cleaned by the sea water and under the burning sun.

An essential yet ubiquitous ingredient that I adore is the intensely aromatic dried wild flowering oregano, *origanum*, which means in Greek "the joy of the mountains," the one herb I prefer dried to fresh. I have never found better anywhere in the world. But when I land in Greece, I crave a simple salad that includes the best quality Kalamata olives and feta cheese I can find marinated in a little of that dried oregano, some thyme or mint maybe, and the deepest, darkest, most pungent olive oil. I dip slices of bread into the salad and eat it with my chilled glass of wine; my mouth waters just thinking about it!

Of course, being French, I don't believe in eating food without wine to accompany it and in the course of the last 10 to 15 years, Greece has been producing some unique quality wines. One of their most famous is the Samos Vin Doux, a sweet wine that is the oldest in Greece and can now be found in some of the finest restaurants in the world.

IN A FEW WORDS, WHAT DOES GREECE MEAN TO YOU?

Greece is a cherished little piece of heaven to me, home to some of my dearest friends and one of my restaurants, L'Avenue, at the intimate yet elegant Metropolitan Hotel in Athens.

The head chef at L'Avenue, Ilias Kariotoglou, is a dear friend who worked with me for years at The Waterside Inn in the UK, and before that we combined forces on cuisine at Celebrity Cruises. Ilias has opened my eyes to many hidden wonders, in particular some restaurant gems in Athens.

I find the contrasts in Athens spellbinding, the manic energy of modern life throbbing to the backbeat of its rich, ancient past. I love the city and its buzz but my heart longs for the simplicity and peace of the villages more. It is a country dominated by water like no other, and in fact has the bluest sea I have ever seen.
I love exploring the tiny restaurants tucked away in olive tree–clad hills and taking little boat trips with friends and family in tow. A favorite island dish I have enjoyed is pan-fried whole red mullet "savoro-style" with vinegar, sultanas, and rosemary.

WHAT IS YOUR FONDEST MEMORY OF GREECE?

I have spent a couple of memorable summers at Porto Heli in the eastern Peloponnese. It's a beautiful and magical area, at once cosmopolitan, sophisticated with stunning hotels and shops, yet centered on a simple, picturesque fishing village with the very sparse ruins of the ancient city of Halieis across the way.
The place is a little gem and I have observed its increasing popularity as it seems to be helping spearhead the recovery of Greece from its recent tourism and economic crisis. Porto Heli thrives with culture and vibrant color and is both wild and elegant at the same time. It is a place of peace, where everyday worries and problems seem to melt away into the sea. Here, I enjoy holidays filled with old friends and new encounters, relaxing by the pool where we might plan simple outings by boat during the day to find isolated sandy beaches, but I can't keep out of the kitchen for long, so here you will find me, rustling up dinner to the tune of the scents and inspirations of this enchanting piece of heaven.

Whole Red Mullet Savoro-Style

Σαβόρο · Savoro

This recipe is dedicated to my dear friend, Ilias Kariotoglou, head chef at L'Avenue, Metropolitan Hotel in Athens. If red mullet is unavailable you may use perch or trout. When slicing the garlic, be sure to remove the green shoot, as this can taste bitter. For a tasty twist, you can grate some bottarga (cured fish roe) on top. If you like, serve this fish with a light salad of halved green grapes, slivered green onions, parsley, tomato, and lemon zest.

1 Place the flour in a shallow dish. Pat the fish dry thoroughly and roll them in the flour to lightly coat. Shake to remove excess flour.

2 Heat the oil in a large skillet over medium heat. Slowly pan-fry the mullet for 2 minutes on each side and then take out and drain on paper towels. Lower the heat and add the garlic slices to the pan; cook briefly. Add the cherry tomatoes, sugar, and tomato paste and give a little stir. Next, add the raisins and rosemary. Add the vinegar and stir, scraping up any browned bits on the bottom of the pan. Pour in ¾ cup/200 ml of water, bring to a boil, then reduce the heat and let simmer for 5 to 7 minutes. Add the lemon juice and season with salt and cayenne pepper. Once the sauce coats the back of a spoon, remove the pan from the heat. Place the red mullet on a plate, pour the sauce over them, and serve.

Ingredients *(Serves 6)*

* ½ cup/70 g all-purpose flour
* 6 medium red mullet, cleaned, scaled, and gutted
* 1¼ cups/300 ml olive oil
* 1 garlic clove, sliced
* 5 oz/150 g cherry tomatoes (cut into quarters)
* 1 tbsp sugar
* 1 tsp tomato paste
* 2 cups/290 g raisins or currants
* 4–5 sprigs fresh rosemary
* 1⅓ cups/320 ml good-quality red wine vinegar
* Juice of ½ lemon
* Salt
* Cayenne pepper

This dish, which resembles the Venetian sardelle in saor, *may date to Byzantine or even Roman times, given its sweet and sour accents they were so fond of. In the days before refrigeration, it was an ideal way of preserving leftover fish, and considered such a delicacy that housewives would cook more than the family could eat at one sitting. In the 19th century, on seafaring islands like Ithaca, women would ship boxes of it to their husbands and sons who worked on the Danube riverboats. In other words, Savoro will keep—but why not gobble it up right away?*

HRH PRINCE NIKOLAOS

Prince Nikolaos was born in 1969, in Rome. His parents, King Constantine and Queen Anne-Marie, had moved there following the Colonels' Coup in Greece in 1967. In 1975 the family settled in London, where Nikolaos was home-educated before attending the Hellenic College of London. While studying international relations at Brown University in Rhode Island, he took a year off to join the British Army on a Short Service Limited Commission with the Royal Scots Dragoon Guards. After graduating in 1993, Nikolaos worked for Fox News in New York, NatWest Markets, and King Constantine's family office. Since 2003 he has been active in consulting.

For the past three years, Prince Nikolaos has dedicated himself to photography, aiming to capture the artful beauty that exists in nature and everyday surroundings. In November 2015 he participated in a group exhibition at Christie's in London. In March 2016 his photography was featured at the New York Times *"Art for Tomorrow" Conference in Doha, Qatar. He sits on the Board of Knightsbridge Schools International and is an active member of Symplefsi, a Greek nonprofit volunteer organization that supports local communities on remote islands. Prince Nikolaos and his wife, Princess Tatiana, were married in 2010. Three years later, they moved to Athens.*

WHAT IS YOUR FAVORITE GREEK FOOD?

Since moving to Greece in 2013, I have rediscovered the delicious tastes of fresh organic produce—everything from the land and sea in Greece is so much more abundant in flavor than anywhere else.

What makes me happiest about it is the smile I see on my wife's face every time we go to the market together and her excitement, which is contagious, when she comes home with a new seasonal product like wild asparagus—it is as if she is bringing back hidden treasures.

My favorites have to be Tatiana's *kolokythakia makaronada* (pasta with zucchini) or a plate of hot steaming *yiouvetsi* (a baked meat dish cooked with orzo) or *kotosoupa avgolemono* (egg-lemon soup with chicken) on a cold winter's night at home or up in the mountains of Zagorohoria. I love the simplest but tastiest potato salad—hand-crushed hot baked potato topped with extra-virgin oil from Mani, sea salt flakes from Messolonghi, and parsley.

During hot summer afternoons, fresh sea urchins, marinated *gavros* (anchovies) with a sprinkling of chile peppers, and Greek tomatoes, which are of unparalleled taste and color, enjoyed with ice-cold raki from Crete, make for the perfect summer lunch shared with friends and family.

IN A FEW WORDS, WHAT DOES GREECE MEAN TO YOU?

In a single word: everything. It is my home country and the very core of my identity. Even though I was raised abroad, Greece has shaped me into who I am today in so many ways. It is a place I always dreamed would be my home and now I am grateful that it finally is. There is a unique light ever present in Greece—it is in fact this light that inspires me every time I pick up my camera to try and capture some of the most beautiful landscapes I have seen.

WHAT IS YOUR FONDEST MEMORY OF GREECE?

Exiting the church with my wife on our wedding day in Spetses is by far my fondest memory. The next has to be the night in 2004 when Greece won the European Cup for the first time. The euphoria of the people on the streets was palpable. Everyone was absolutely united. The magic of this unity served as an introduction to the celebratory mood that engulfed Greece that summer, as we still had the Olympics to host.

I am equally grateful for the everyday memories of life here, particularly the ones I make when encountering people and places for the first time.

Traveling extensively with Tatiana, I feel privileged to get acquainted with some of Greece's many treasures that often go unnoticed. As an active member of a nonprofit volunteer organization, I have had the opportunity to travel to some of the most remote islands—these islands and their residents have granted me some of my fondest memories.

Baked Beef Casserole with Orzo

Γιουβέτσι · Yiouvetsi

Orzo is a favorite type of pasta in Greece and any dish with it is called yiouvetsi, *which is the name of the clay pot it is traditionally cooked in.* Graviera *is a hard, light-yellow cheese with a nutty flavor. If you can't find it, you can substitute* Gruyère.

Ingredients *(Serves 4 to 5)*

* 1¾ lb/800 g boneless beef stewing meat or lamb shoulder, trimmed and cut into large cubes
* Salt and freshly ground black pepper
* ¼ cup/60 ml olive oil
* 2 onions, finely chopped
* 1 bay leaf
* 1 cinnamon stick
* 1 whole clove
* 2 allspice berries
* 2½ tbsp tomato paste
* 2 garlic cloves, finely chopped
* 1 tsp sweet paprika
* 10 tbsp/150 ml red wine
* 4½ cups/1 L beef broth, plus extra if needed
* 7 oz/200 g tomatoes, halved, seeded, and grated
* 1 tsp sugar
* 11 oz/320 g orzo
* 2 oz/55 g *graviera* cheese, grated
* 3 tbsp unsalted butter
* 1 tbsp finely chopped fresh parsley

1 Preheat the oven to 325°F/165°C.

2 Season the meat with salt and pepper to taste. Heat the oil in a large pot or Dutch oven over high heat, add the meat, and brown it on all sides. Lower the heat to medium and add the onions, sautéing them until they're translucent.

3 Wrap the bay leaf, cinnamon stick, clove, and allspice berries in a small bundle of cheesecloth (or pound them and place in a tea ball). Add the spice bundle, garlic, tomato paste, and paprika to the pot and give them a good stir. Pour in the wine and cook until it has boiled down by about two-thirds. Add the broth, grated tomatoes, and sugar. Bring to a boil, cover the pot, and transfer it to the oven. Cook for 2 hours.

4 Increase the oven temperature to 425°F/220°C. Remove the pot from the oven, remove the spice bundle, and stir in the orzo. Sprinkle the *graviera* over the top. Return the pot to the oven, uncovered, and cook for another 15 minutes, adding extra broth if necessary. When the orzo seems done, finish off the dish by stirring in the butter and 2 ice cubes to keep the orzo from overcooking. Sprinkle with the parsley and serve.

Orzo Casserole with Shrimp, Tomatoes & Saffron

Γιουβέτσι με γαρίδες, ντομάτα και κρόκο Κοζάνης
Yiouvetsi me garides, domata kai kroko Kozanis

Because I couldn't make up my mind which of these yiouvetsi *dishes I like better, I decided to include them both as among my all-time favorites. This recipe makes more shrimp bisque than you'll need for the casserole; refrigerate the rest and enjoy it as a soup on its own.*

Ingredients *(Serves 4)*

Shrimp Bisque

- 12 colossal shrimp, fresh or frozen (about 1 lb/500 g total)
- ¼ cup/60 ml olive oil
- 1¾ cups/200 g coarsely chopped onion
- 1 cup/120 g coarsely chopped carrot
- 2 garlic cloves
- 2 tbsp tomato paste
- 7 tbsp/100 ml brandy
- ⅓ cup/80 ml dry white wine
- 6½ cups/1.5 l water or fish stock
- 2 bay leaves

Note: If you can't find uncleaned shrimp, you can use a fish stock cube instead.

I *For the shrimp bisque:* Peel and devein the shrimp, reserving the shells and heads (if the shrimp were purchased with the heads on). Place the peeled shrimp in a bowl, cover, and refrigerate. Heat the oil in a large skillet over medium heat, add the onions, carrots, and garlic, and cook, stirring, until the vegetables are softened and the onions are translucent. Add the shrimp shells and heads and stir to coat with oil.
Add the tomato paste and stir to incorporate. Add the brandy, remove the pan from the heat, and flambé it. Quench the flame with the wine, then return the pan to the heat and cook to evaporate a bit.
Add the water and bay leaves and simmer for 40 minutes. Working in batches, process the bisque in a blender and then strain it through a large fine-mesh strainer set over a bowl. Discard the solids and set 1 cup/240 ml of the bisque aside; refrigerate the rest.

2 *For the casserole:* Heat about two-thirds of the oil in a large nonstick frying pan over medium-high heat, add the shrimp, and cook for about 1 minute per side. Transfer the shrimp to a bowl. Add the grated onion to the pan and cook for a few minutes, then add the garlic, and finally stir in the orzo and cook for a couple of minutes. Pour in the ouzo. Add the reserved 1 cup/240 ml shrimp bisque, the broth, grated tomatoes, sugar, and saffron. Simmer for about 10 minutes. Add the butter and the remaining oil and season with salt and pepper to taste. Return the shrimp to the pan and let them heat through, then sprinkle with parsley and serve.

Casserole

* ¼ cup/60 ml olive oil
* 1 large white onion, grated
* 1 garlic clove
* 7 oz/200 g orzo
* 3½ tbsp ouzo
* 2½ cups/600 ml vegetable or chicken broth
* 2 tomatoes, peeled, seeded, and grated
* ½ tsp sugar
* ½ tsp saffron threads, moistened with a few tablespoons of the broth
* 4 tbsp/55 g unsalted butter
* Salt and freshly ground black pepper
* 1 tbsp finely chopped fresh parsley

Egg-Lemon Soup with Chicken

Κοτόσουπα με αυγολέμονο · Kotosoupa me avgolemono

If you can, choose a free-range, organic chicken for this recipe; it really makes a difference. Many versions of this recipe call for cooking the rice directly in the chicken broth, but it can soak up all the broth, creating a sort of chicken risotto. Cooking the rice separately gives the soup a better consistency.

Ingredients *(Serves 4 to 5)*

* 1 (3- to 3½-lb/1.4- to 1.6 kg) chicken, giblets discarded
* 2 onions, halved
* 2 carrots
* 4 celery stalks, halved
* 5 or 6 sprigs fresh parsley
* 4 peppercorns
* Salt
* 1 cup/200 g medium- or long-grain white rice
* Lemon wedges

Egg and Lemon Sauce

* 2 large eggs, at room temperature
* Juice of 1 to 2 lemons
* 1 tsp cornstarch (optional)

1 Place the chicken in a large pot, cover with water, and bring to a boil. Skim the scum from the surface until the water is clear again. Add the onions, carrots, celery, parsley, peppercorns, and a few pinches of salt and bring to a boil again, then lower the heat and simmer until the chicken is tender and cooked through, about 1¼ hours.

2 While the chicken is cooking, rinse the rice, then place it in a small saucepan with 2 cups water. Cover, bring to a boil, then reduce the heat and simmer until tender, about 15 minutes (follow package directions, as times may vary). Set aside.

3 Remove the chicken to a platter so the juices won't escape. Strain the broth through a fine-mesh strainer set over a bowl, pressing on the vegetables to get the most out of all the ingredients. Discard the vegetables and pour the broth back into the pot.
Pull the chicken meat off the bones, dice it, and add to the broth.

4 *For the egg and lemon sauce:* Simply beat the eggs in a bowl and whisk in the lemon juice. (If you prefer to thicken the sauce, first blend the cornstarch with just enough water to make a paste and add it to the egg and lemon mix. This reduces the risk of curdling but if you're careful, this won't happen.)
Very slowly add a little of the warm (not hot!) broth to the egg mixture. Once you have added about half of the broth, you can pour the mixture back into the pot. Warm gently—if not, you will end up with scrambled eggs.
Do not let the soup boil. Add the cooked rice, season with salt and pepper to taste, and serve with lemon wedges. Enjoy!

Tatiana's Zucchini Carbonara

Κολοκυθάκια μακαρονάδα · Kolokythakia makaronada

If you can't find kefalotyri *or* graviera *cheese, you can substitute Parmesan or Pecorino Romano, or you can use a blend of these cheeses.*

Ingredients

(Serves 2—or 1 very hungry husband!)

- 3 tbsp extra-virgin olive oil
- 1 red onion, diced
- 1 lb/455 g medium zucchini, shredded (about 3½ cups)
- Salt and freshly ground black pepper
- 2½ oz/70 g *kefalotyri* cheese, grated (¾ cup)
- 1 oz/30 g *graviera* cheese, grated (¼ cup), plus extra for serving
- 2 egg yolks, at room temperature
- 7 oz/200 g spaghetti or fusilli

1 Heat the oil in a large, heavy skillet over medium heat. Add the onion and cook, stirring, until pale golden, about 2 minutes. Add the zucchini and cook until it begins to color, about 10 minutes. Season with salt and pepper to taste. Remove from the heat.

2 Meanwhile, combine the *kefalotyri* and *graviera* in a large bowl, add the egg yolks, and beat with a fork. Season with salt and pepper. Bring a large pot of water to a boil and season with salt, then add the pasta and cook until just al dente, stirring occasionally.

3 Drain, keeping a spoonful of the water to add to the egg mixture (this is a little trick you can use with any pasta sauce, as it helps to thicken the sauce). Add half of the pasta to the egg mixture and toss to coat. Add the other half of the pasta to the pan with the zucchini and toss to coat. Throw the pasta and zucchini into the big bowl, toss it all together, and it is ready. (The heat from the pasta will cook the eggs. Dividing it up slows the process down so you don't end up with scrambled eggs.) Season with more salt and pepper to taste and serve with extra cheese if you wish.

i

Although shredded zucchini cooks faster, you can instead slice it into ¼-inch/6-mm-thick rounds. As a change from regular wheat pasta, you can use spelt or rice pasta, or even Greek chickpea flour fusilli, which is delicious and nutritious.

NIKOS ALIAGAS

Nikos Aliagas was born in Paris in 1969 to Greek parents. After graduating with a degree in modern French literature from the Sorbonne, he began his media career with Radio France International, moving to Radio Notre-Dame in 1992. Meanwhile, he also edited a Greek cultural magazine and presented a Greek language radio program for an Armenian radio station. Nikos, who speaks five languages, joined Euronews in 1993, spending the next six years as a core political reporter with a special focus on Greece and Cyprus, while also presenting the news for Tele Monte Carlo. In 2001 Nikos joined channel TF1, where he still presents the biggest shows on French TV. Besides his television career, for Europe1 radio Nikos interviews leading international personalities in the arts and the academic world. He has published several books on Greek civilization and is a passionate photographer. Nikos finds charity work most rewarding and is a founding patron of the cystic fibrosis charity Association Grégory Lemarchal and of Wheeling Around the World, which helps facilitate travel for people with disabilities. He was named a chevalier of the Order of Arts and Letters, one of the most distinguished awards in France, and he also had a stamp dedicated to him in Greece.

WHAT IS YOUR FAVORITE GREEK FOOD?

My favorite Greek product, the salted and sun-dried roe of the gray mullet, comes from my home town, Messolonghi. Also known as bottarga, in Greek it is called *avgotaraho*. It has an intense taste (almost like the sea itself) and is full of nutrients, too, an ideal *meze*.

IN A FEW WORDS, WHAT DOES GREECE MEAN TO YOU?

As a Greek who was born and raised in Paris by two proud Greek parents, I grew up feeling Greece in my DNA. Greece is so much more than its natural beauty, its history, and its philosophy. It is a way of thinking, of existing. It is like an archetype imprinted in the collective unconscious of all Greeks, which defines them in a way that goes way beyond the visible world that surrounds us. Therefore, as you can imagine, Greece means a lot to me—the air that I smell, my connection with myself and others, spirituality, the place where I come from . . . the list is endless.

WHAT IS YOUR FONDEST MEMORY OF GREECE?

Greece is associated with my dearest and fondest memories and life experiences so far. If I had to choose one, it would be the christening of our daughter Agathe at the small monastery of Saint Agathe in Aitoloakarnania (central Greece) in July 2013. Saint Agathe is the protector of the area and is worshiped in a profound spiritual way by the local people, who organize a three-day fete every August in order to honor her. From a very young age I've participated actively in the fete, which involves altering your conscious state through a collective experience of praying, singing, and dancing in such a way that you feel connected to the Divine. This strong tradition is a kind of personal catharsis.

My participation in these annual fetes reminds me of the meaning of life and gives me strength and direction. In this way, Agathe's christening was an intensely spiritual and happy experience for me, a wonderful moment that we shared with the people that we love, at the place I love most. It was a beautiful afternoon full of Greek flavors, smells, songs, laughter, and tears. Following the ceremony, we danced under the maple trees outside the monastery and then continued our celebration at Stamna, a picturesque village where my father was born. Speaking of Greek food and delicacies, you need to try the suckling pork roasted on the spit at Stamna; it may be the best in the country.

Greek Baked Macaroni

Παστίτσιο · Pastitsio

Pastitsio is classic comfort food, and something that children of all ages seem to crave. Graviera is a hard, light-yellow cheese with a nutty flavor. If you can't find it, you can substitute Gruyère.

Ingredients *(Serves 8 to 10)*

Meat Sauce

* 2 carrots, peeled and chopped
* 2 onions, chopped
* 1 celery stalk, chopped
* 2 garlic cloves, peeled
* ½ cup/120 ml olive oil
* 1¼ lb/600 g ground beef
* ½ cup/120 ml dry red wine
* 2 cups/360 g chopped tomatoes (canned is fine)
* 2 cups/480 ml beef broth or chicken broth
* 1 tbsp tomato paste
* 1 tsp sweet paprika
* 5–6 sprigs fresh thyme (or ½ tsp dried thyme)
* 1 bay leaf
* 1 cinnamon stick

1 *For the meat sauce:* Place the carrots, onions, celery, and garlic in a food processor or blender and process until very finely chopped but not mushy.

2 Heat the olive oil in a large skillet over medium heat, add the ground beef, and cook until there's no sign of pink.
When it's the color of a well-done steak, stir it with a wooden spoon until the meat breaks up into little rice-sized particles.
Add the finely chopped vegetables and cook for 5 minutes until they soften. Pour in the wine and cook until it evaporates.

3 Add the chopped tomatoes, broth, tomato paste, paprika, thyme sprigs, bay leaf, and cinnamon stick and simmer over medium heat until the sauce has thickened, about 2 hours. Remove the thyme sprigs, bay leaf, and cinnamon stick.

4 *For the béchamel:* While the meat sauce is cooking, heat the milk in a small saucepan. Melt the butter in a separate saucepan over medium heat and add the flour, whisking all the while until you have a smooth paste. Add the hot milk, whisking constantly, over very low heat until it thickens. Season with salt, pepper, and nutmeg to taste. Set aside.

5 Preheat the oven to 350°F/185°C. Butter an 11 by 15-inch/28 by 38-cm baking dish and set aside.

6 Bring a large pot of water to a boil and season with salt; add the pasta and cook until al dente. Drain in a colander, season with salt and pepper while in the colander, tossing it gently, and return it to the pot. Add the meat sauce, half the béchamel, the eggs, and half the *graviera* and mix well.

7 Empty the contents of the pot into the baking dish and pour the rest of the béchamel over it. Even it out with a spatula moistened with water and sprinkle with the remaining *graviera* and the breadcrumbs. Bake until golden brown, 35 to 40 minutes. Let the pastitsio cool for 10 to 15 minutes and serve. (Allowing the pastitsio to rest before you dig into it makes cutting and serving it easier.)

Béchamel

* 6½ cups/1.5 l milk
* 10 tbsp/150 g unsalted butter
* 1 cup plus 2 tbsp/150 g all-purpose flour
* Salt and freshly ground white pepper
* Ground nutmeg

* 1 lb/455 g (1 packet) long macaroni, thick spaghetti, or bucatini
* 2 eggs
* 7 oz/200 g *graviera* cheese, grated
* 2 tbsp dried breadcrumbs

Pumpkin Pie

Κολοκυθόπιτα γλυκιά · Kolokythopita glykia

Ingredients *(Serves 8 to 10)*

* 2½ lb/1.2 kg pumpkin, peeled and seeded
* 1 cup plus 1 tbsp/180 g coarse semolina flour
* 1 cup/200 g packed brown sugar
* ¾ cup/100 g crushed walnuts
* ⅔ cup/100 g currants
* 2 tbsp ground cinnamon, plus extra for sprinkling
* 1 tsp ground cloves
* 1 packet phyllo pastry, about 20–25 sheets
* 14 tbsp/200 g unsalted butter, melted
* Confectioners' sugar

1 Preheat the oven to 350°F/180°C.

2 Coarsely grate the pumpkin into a colander and squeeze out as much liquid as possible with your hands. (Or if you're not in a rush, cover the grated pumpkin and leave it to drain overnight.) Place the pumpkin in a bowl and add the semolina, sugar, walnuts, currants, cinnamon, and cloves.

3 Lay 1 phyllo sheet on the counter and brush with melted butter, then fold it in half lengthwise and spread 3 to 4 tablespoons of the pumpkin filling along the bottom of the folded phyllo, leaving 0.5 inch/1.25 cm or so unfilled at each end and at the bottom. Roll it loosely into a long cylinder, then curl it into a spiral, like a snail and place it in the center of a round baking pan, about 14 inches/35 cm in diameter. Butter, fill, and roll a second phyllo sheet and curl this phyllo stick around the first one in the pan, placing one end right up against the end of the first stick.
Repeat with the other phyllo sheets until you have used up all the filling, forming a large spiral. Brush the surface of the pie with any remaining melted butter.
Bake until the crust is golden, about 40 minutes. Serve hot or cold, sprinkled with confectioners' sugar and a little cinnamon.

Spaghetti with Red-Hot Chile Peppers, Bottarga & Lime

Μακαρονάδα με αυγοτάραχο · Makaronada me avgotaraho

This recipe was suggested by the man who may know bottarga better than anyone in Greece. Like Nikos Aliagas, Zafiris Trikalinos comes from the Messolonghi lagoon area, home to many of the gray mullet that produce this delectable roe. Preserving it has been a family business for three generations. Zafiris perfected the technique and the Trikalinos name has come to be identified with the product, which is available in select shops around the world. It comes sealed with beeswax to keep it fresh. You can slice it through the wax, but don't be fooled; it's not edible.

1 Bring a large pot of water to a boil and season with salt, then add the pasta and cook until al dente. Drain the pasta, reserving 1 cup of the pasta cooking water.

2 Heat the olive oil in a heavy saucepan over medium heat. Add the chiles and garlic and let warm through. Add the reserved pasta water, lime zest and juice, and chives, and cook until the sauce thickens slightly. Add the spaghetti, stir, and remove from the heat. Add the Parmesan and the sliced bottarga and mix well. Serve.

i *For a more intense flavor, replace the Parmesan with bottarga powder.*

Ingredients *(Serves 4)*

* Salt
* 1 lb/500 g spaghetti
* 2 tbsp extra-virgin olive oil
* 4 small red hot dried chile peppers, smashed, or red pepper flakes
* ½ garlic clove, smashed
* Grated zest and juice of 2 limes
* 2 tbsp chopped fresh chives
* ¼ cup grated Parmesan cheese
* 30 thin slices bottarga

NOBU MATSUHISA

Nobuyuki Matsuhisa—known simply as Nobu—is the acclaimed and highly influential chef/proprietor of Nobu and Matsuhisa restaurants, located across five continents. Born and raised in Saitama, Japan, Nobu served an apprenticeship in Tokyo before he moved to Peru to open a sushi bar. As a classically trained sushi chef, Nobu was challenged by the new culture and regional ingredients, which kindled his inventive style, known today as Nobu Style. After further stops in Argentina, Japan, and Alaska, he settled down in Los Angeles, where he opened his first restaurant, Matsuhisa Beverly Hills, in January 1987. Matsuhisa was an instant success and became a magnet for food lovers and celebrities alike. It was here that his friendship and business relationship with actor and director Robert De Niro began. Together they opened the first Nobu in New York City in 1994 with restaurateur Drew Nieporent. Nobu currently operates 33 Nobu and six Matsuhisa restaurants around the world.

WHAT IS YOUR FAVORITE GREEK FOOD?
Simple food, like Greek salad and fresh fish on the grill with extra-virgin Greek olive oil.

IN A FEW WORDS, WHAT DOES GREECE MEAN TO YOU?
Greece is a beautiful country with unique islands and coastline, but it is also the birthplace of a great civilization.

WHAT IS YOUR FONDEST MEMORY OF GREECE?
The uniqueness of the Greek islands like Mykonos and Santorini. The white houses, the whitewashed pedestrian streets, and the beautiful sunsets.

Sardines with Wasabi Ponzu

Σαρδέλες με Wasabi Ponzu · Sardeles me Wasabi Ponzu

1 Sprinkle the sardines with some salt and let them sit for 5 minutes. Wipe off the salt, along with any liquid, and put the fillets in a shallow dish. Add 10 tbsp/150 ml of the cold rice-wine vinegar and let sit for about 3 minutes. Remove the fillets from the rice-wine vinegar and dry them well in order to stop them from "cooking."

2 *For the karasisumiso* and *onion wasabi ponzu:* Combine the *den miso*, 2 tbsp/30 ml rice-wine vinegar, and *karashi* in a bowl. In a separate bowl, make the onion wasabi ponzu: Mix the rice-wine vinegar and the soy sauce. Add the sunflower oil and stir, then add the onion cubes. Add the pickled wasabi and pureed garlic and stir.

3 Place the sardines on a big plate and season them with the onion wasabi *ponzu* and *karasisumiso* as shown in the photo. Garnish with chives, cilantro, and carrot and serve.

Ingredients *(Serves 1)*

- 5 sardines
- 10 tbsp/150 ml rice-wine vinegar
- Salt

Karasisumiso

- 6 ½ tbsp/100 ml *den miso*
- 4 tsp *karashi*
- 2 tbsp/30 ml rice-wine vinegar

Onion wasabi ponzu

- 1 white onion, diced
- 3 tsp rice-wine vinegar
- 1 ½ tsp soy sauce
- 2 tbsp/30 g pickled wasabi
- 4 tsp/20 ml sunflower oil
- 4 tsp/20 ml *ponzu*
- 1 garlic clove (pureed)
- Chives, cilantro, shredded carrots for garnish

If you want to prepare your own den miso, use 1½ cups/350 g caster sugar, 2 cups/450 g white miso, *⅗ cup/150 ml* sake, *and ⅗ cup/150 ml* mirin.

OLYMPIA DUKAKIS

Olympia Dukakis is an American actress whose award-winning career spans stage, screen, and television. Her performance in Moonstruck *earned her an Academy Award for Best Supporting Actress. She has appeared in more than 60 feature and short films, most recently* 7 Chinese Brothers, Cloudburst, *and* The Infiltrator. *Her television career includes* Tales of the City, More Tales of the City, Further Tales of the City, Bored to Death, *and* The Last of the Blonde Bombshells. *And her theater work, both in the United States and in London, ranges from the acclaimed one-woman show* Rose to Credible Witness to The Marriage of Bette and Boo. *She has performed in more than 130 productions Off Broadway and regionally. Olympia received the Lifetime Achievement Award from the Greek America Foundation and the National Arts Club Medal of Honor, and was recently honored with a star on the Hollywood Walk of Fame.*

WHAT IS YOUR FONDEST MEMORY OF GREECE?

My favorite memory of Greece comes from the '60s—walking in the streets, listening and talking to all the people. Other favorites: performing *Rose* in Athens, and visiting my mother's and father's villages and learning about where they came from.

Fried Squid

Καλαμαράκια τηγανιτά · Kalamarakia tiganita

Fried squid, fresh or frozen, whole baby ones or larger ones cut in rings, are among the most popular dishes in any seaside taverna. In some more upmarket restaurants, you'll find them accompanied by a pesto sauce, which elevates them to another realm of deliciousness.

1 *For the pesto:* Zap the basil, pine nuts, and salt in a food processor for a few seconds. With the processor running, drizzle in the oil until you have a luscious, almost smooth sauce. Add the Parmesan and garlic and process briefly to blend. Transfer to a small bowl.

2 If using fresh squid, clean them by pulling the heads from the tentacles. Remove and discard the ink sacs, transparent cartilage, and beaks. Wash the squid well and pat dry. If using thawed frozen squid, rinse and pat them dry.

3 Pour enough oil into a large saucepan to reach a depth of about 2 inches/5 cm and heat it to 375°F/190°C. Shake the squid in a bag with the flour and give them another shake when you take them out to remove any excess. Working in batches, fry the squid just until crisp on all sides (too much cooking will toughen them). Drain on paper towels, then serve with the pesto and lemon wedges on the side.

Ingredients *(Serves 4 to 6)*

Pesto

* 1 large bunch fresh basil, thick stems removed
* Handful pine nuts
* Good pinch coarse sea salt
* Extra-virgin olive oil
* 2 garlic cloves, minced
* Handful grated Parmesan cheese

* 2 lb/1 kg small squid, fresh or frozen (thawed)
* About 4 cups/1 l olive oil
* 1 cup/140 g all-purpose flour
* Lemon wedges

Spinach Pie with Greens

Σπανακόπιτα με χόρτα · Spanakopita me horta

In honor of Olympia Dukakis's origins, we chose Cretan recipes for her favorite dishes. In this one, spinach is mixed with an assortment of wild greens for which the island is renowned. If you don't have access to wild greens, use a blend of greens from the market, such as chicory, dandelion, broccoli rabe, curly endive, collards, beet or turnip greens, Swiss chard, or arugula. Try to have a mixture of sweet and bitter, but be careful; bitter greens are not to everyone's taste. As for the pastry, little tricks like a tiny bit of sugar and a dollop of red wine make this dough tastier as well as darker than conventional pie crusts.

1 Preheat the oven to 375°F/190°C.

2 Squeeze the greens and spinach with your hands to crush them and rid them of excess water, then chop them finely and place in a large bowl. Add the onion, green onions, parsley, mint, and dill and toss to combine. Heat the oil in a large skillet over medium heat, add the greens, sugar, and salt and pepper to taste, and cook just until the greens are wilted. Set aside. Mix in the crumbled feta (if using) at this point; it will make the greens a little less dense.

3 *For the pastry:* Place the flour in a bowl, make a well in the center, and add the wine, oil, salt, and a third of the water, swirling the flour into the well with your hand. Add the rest of the water slowly until you have a soft dough and knead it well to make it pliable. Separate the dough into 2 balls, one slightly larger than the other, and roll the larger one out on a lightly floured surface until it measures about 12 by 16 inches/ 30 by 40 cm.

Ingredients *(Serves 8 to 10)*

- 2 lb/1 kg assorted wild greens, washed and picked over
- 1 lb/500 g spinach
- 1 onion, finely chopped
- 1 bunch green onions, white and light green parts, finely chopped
- 3 tbsp finely chopped fresh parsley
- 3 tbsp finely chopped fresh mint
- 3 tbsp finely chopped fresh dill or fennel fronds
- ½ cup/120 ml olive oil
- 1 tsp sugar
- Salt and freshly ground black pepper
- 7 oz/200 g feta cheese, crumbled (optional)

Pastry

- 3 cups/450 g bread flour
- ½ cup/120 ml red wine
- ¼ cup/60 ml olive oil, plus extra for the pan
- ½ tsp salt
- 1 cup/240 ml warm water
- Beaten egg yolk or milk (optional)

4 Oil a 9 by 13-inch/25 by 35-cm baking pan, line it with the pastry and place the sautéed greens on top of it. Roll out the second piece of dough to fit the pan and place it on top, folding over the edges to seal. With a sharp knife, score the top into serving portions, and if desired paint with a little beaten egg yolk or milk. Bake for about 1 hour. Let cool slightly, then serve.

i *If you'd like, you can substitute store-bought phyllo dough for the homemade dough. Line the baking pan with 4 or 5 sheets of phyllo, brushing each one with a little oil as you place it in the pan. Spread the greens on top and cover with 4 or 5 more sheets of phyllo, brushing each one with oil. Cut the pie into serving portions, paint the top sheet with oil and bake until the crust is golden brown, about 1 hour.*

In the Heraklio and Chania farmers' markets you can find small bunches of wild greens sold for pies and stews. The mixture varies with the time of year, but it can include wild carrot, leek, wild fennel, chard, or perhaps salsify tops, sorrel, tordylium, chervil, corn poppy leaves, plantain, dandelion, and mustard greens, among other tender shoots.

Octopus with Lemon Sauce

Χταπόδι λεμονάτο · Htapodi lemonato

This recipe from Crete is about as simple as it gets. Octopus with an oil and vinegar dressing is very common all over Greece. Cooking it with oil and lemon makes for a delightful change.

1 Rinse octopus (fresh or frozen and thawed) and place it in a nonstick medium saucepan with the olive oil.

2 Cover and cook over low heat; the octopus will cook in its own juices. When its liquid has evaporated, lift out the octopus and cut it into bite-size pieces, discarding the beak and scraping the hood clean (if fresh). Return it to the pot along with the juice of 2 or 3 lemons and simmer until tender.

3 Serve at room temperature, sprinkled with dried oregano.

Ingredients *(Serves 4 to 6)*

* 2½ lb/1.2 kg octopus, fresh or frozen (thawed)
* 2–3 tbsp extra-virgin olive oil
* Juice of 2 to 3 lemons
* Dried oregano

PETER MINAKI

Greek Canadian Peter Minaki is the creator of the popular food blog Kalofagas—Greek Food and Beyond. Kalofagas *is the Greek word for "gourmet." Peter started the blog because he wanted to introduce the world to the delicious depths and diversity of Greek cuisine, and his posts are a balance of traditional and modernized recipes and his own unique recipes. Apart from writing two cookbooks,* Everything Mediterranean *and* The Big Book of Mediterranean Recipes, *Peter is a supper-club host and frequent contributor to InsideToronto.com, Canadian and international magazines, and websites. He returns to his roots in Greece every summer.*

WHAT IS YOUR FAVORITE GREEK FOOD?
Depends on the season but let's go with Greek comfort food. You can never go wrong with *kolokithakia yemista* (stuffed zucchini) with *avgolemono* sauce.

IN A FEW WORDS, WHAT DOES GREECE MEAN TO YOU?
My visits to Greece keep me connected with my heritage, family, and friends, and something within me comes alive. Greece is magical!

WHAT IS YOUR FONDEST MEMORY OF GREECE?
Sipping morning and afternoon Greek coffee with my *pappou* (grandfather) in Thessaloniki when I was in my early 20s.

Slow-Roasted Leg of Lamb

Αρνάκι ψητό σε σιγανό φούρνο • Arnaki psito se sigano fourno

Ingredients *(Serves 8 to 10)*

* 1 bone-in leg of lamb or 2 short-cut legs of lamb (6 to 8 lb/2.7 to 3.6 kg total), trimmed
* 1 head garlic, cloves peeled and cut into slivers
* ½ cup/120 ml extra-virgin olive oil, plus extra for drizzling on the lamb and potatoes
* 5 tsp fine sea salt
* 2 tsp freshly ground black pepper
* 2 tsp sweet paprika
* 2 onions, peeled and quartered
* 10 sprigs fresh thyme
* 2–3 sprigs fresh rosemary
* 2–3 tsp dried oregano
* 2–3 bay leaves
* 1 cup/240 ml dry white wine
* Juice of 2 lemons
* 4 lb/1.8 kg potatoes

1 Preheat the oven to 550°F/290°C.

2 Using a paring knife, poke a hole into the lamb, then slip in a sliver of garlic. Repeat and insert as many slivers of garlic as you can into the leg.

3 Drizzle oil over the leg and season it with the salt, pepper, and paprika. Place the leg of lamb in a large roasting pan (the leg should just fit in the pan) and roast uncovered until browned, 10 to 15 minutes, then flip the leg over and roast for another 10 to 15 minutes.

4 Remove the lamb from the oven and reduce the heat to 350°F/180°C. Place the quartered onions around the lamb, add the thyme, rosemary, oregano, and any remaining garlic slivers, then pour in the wine, oil, and lemon juice. Add enough hot water to cover a third of the lamb.

5 Cover the pan and roast the lamb for 2 hours, basting the lamb after 1 hour. Flip the leg of lamb and cover it again, add more water, along with salt and pepper, if necessary, and continue to roast it until the lamb is deep brown, the bones are exposed, and the meat is starting to separate from the bone, about 1 hour. Remove the lamb from the oven, baste with the liquid, and let rest.

6 While the lamb is roasting, peel and quarter the potatoes. Place them in a large baking pan, drizzle with oil, and season with salt and pepper to taste. When the lamb is done, pour enough pan juices from the lamb to come up a third of the way on the potatoes and toss to coat. Taste, adjust seasonings, crank the oven up to 450°F/230°C, and roast the potatoes until fork-tender, 35 to 40 minutes (the lamb will stay warm covered in the roasting pan on the stovetop). Serve the lamb with the potatoes.

Phyllo Cigars with Bougatsa Cream

Πούρα από φύλλο με κρέμα μπουγάτσας · *Poura apo fyllo me krema bougatsas*

These pastries are delicious with a Greek coffee or a foamy, iced café frappé. *Thick, or country-style, phyllo is called* horiatiko *in Greece. Country-style phyllo leaves are still quite thin, but are sturdier than the kind of phyllo leaves used for baklava. They come in 1-pound/455-g boxes, about eight sheets to a box. If you can't find country-style phyllo, you can use the more readily available thin kind.*

Ingredients *(Makes 45 to 50 cigars)*

Custard

* 12 tbsp/170 g unsalted butter
* 1 cup/140 g fine semolina flour
* ⅔ cup/130 g sugar
* Pinch salt
* 3¼ cups/780 ml whole milk
* 1 tbsp vanilla extract
* Grated zest of ½ orange

Cigars

* 12 (14 by 18-in/36 by 46-cm) sheets country-style phyllo, at room temperature
* 1 tbsp cornstarch mixed with ½ cup/120 ml water
* Oil for frying
* Confectioners' sugar
* Ground cinnamon

1 *For the custard:* Melt the butter in a medium saucepan over medium heat; add the semolina, sugar, and salt; and cook, stirring for a couple of minutes until the butter is absorbed and the semolina is golden but not browned.

2 While whisking, add the milk in a steady stream until all the liquid is absorbed. Cook while stirring for 3 to 4 minutes, until the custard has the texture of loose cream of wheat. Remove from the heat, add the vanilla and orange zest, and stir in. Press plastic wrap over the custard and let cool (do not place the lid on the pot).

3 *For the cigars:* Place a sheet of phyllo on a clean counter and cut it into 4 even pieces, about 7 by 9 inches/17 by 23 cm each. Working with 1 piece at a time, turn it so a short side is facing you and place a tablespoon of custard about ½ inch/12 mm from the bottom.
Spread the custard in a line along the bottom, leaving ½ inch/12 mm at either end. Fold the bottom of the phyllo sheet over the filling, then fold the sides in and roll up until there is 1 inch/2.5 cm of phyllo left.

4 Dip your finger into the cornstarch slurry, wet the top end of the phyllo, and roll it up. Place the cigar on a parchment paper–lined baking sheet. Repeat with the remaining phyllo sheets and filling. (At this point, the cigars may be frozen for future use.)

5 Heat about 1 inch of oil in a large, deep skillet over medium heat and fry the phyllo cigars, a few at a time, until golden on all sides. Drain on a paper-lined baking sheet.

6 Let cool for 5 minutes, then serve (the filling will still be warm). For a final touch, cut in half and dust with confectioners' sugar and cinnamon.

Cheese Croquettes

Κροκέτες με τυρί · Kroketes me tyri

This is an easy appetizer that most people seem to love.

Ingredients *(Makes 8 to 10 croquettes)*

- 4 oz/115 g feta cheese, crumbled (1 cup)
- ¼ cup/35 g all-purpose flour
- 1 egg
- Sesame seeds
- Oil for frying

1 Put the feta and flour in a medium bowl, crack the egg into it and mix with your hands until incorporated. Roll the mixture into 8 to 10 balls, then coat in sesame seeds.

2 Heat about 1 inch of oil in a large, deep skillet, place the cheese balls in the oil, and fry on all sides until golden. Remove with a slotted spoon and drain on paper towels. Serve warm or at room temperature.

RITA WILSON

Multitalented Rita Wilson was born in Los Angeles, to a Greek mother and Bulgarian father. An actress, singer, and film producer, she is best known for My Big Fat Greek Wedding, *a runaway hit that has become the biggest earner in the history of independent movies. Her movie acting credits include roles in* MASH, Sleepless in Seattle, Perfume, It's Complicated, *and many others, and she has guest-starred in TV series like* Law and Order, The Good Wife, Frasier, *and more. She played Roxie in the Broadway revival of* Chicago *in 2006 and acted in* Fish in the Dark *in 2015. In March 2016, she released her second studio album, a self-titled collection of original songs. Rita is active in charity work, raising money for cancer research and children's causes. She is married to actor Tom Hanks and has two children.*

WHAT IS YOUR FAVORITE GREEK FOOD?

The *vassilopita* my mom used to make on New Year's Day. As kids, we would eagerly wait around the table as we helped her brush the dough with butter, while trying to catch her sliding the shiny silver quarter into the egg batter. I also love Kalamata olives and full-fat homemade Greek yogurt, drizzled with Greek honey, which I eat for breakfast every day.

IN A FEW WORDS, WHAT DOES GREECE MEAN TO YOU?

Greece means happiness, a connection to my maternal roots, the freedom the seas offer and impart and to which I can turn during the cold days of winter to bring me to the warmth of a summer day. The people are so warm and have so much integrity. Greeks love their country and their heritage. When I return to Greece it's like I'm meeting up with an old friend who I love. We pick up where we left off as if I never left.

WHAT IS YOUR FONDEST MEMORY OF GREECE?

When I was 16 my parents took me to Greece for the first time. We stayed in Glyfada (a coastal suburb of Athens). I went to Astir Beach every day. I learned to water-ski in Vouliagmeni. At night, we would go to Nine Muses and dance. To this day, the fragrance of a gardenia takes me right back to the flowers that a date could buy you at the club. That summer is etched in my memory as a time and place that illustrated a love of life the Greek people possess.

Greek New Year's Cake

Βασιλόπιτα · Vassilopita

*There is a special ritual observed in the cutting of this cake, which has had a good luck charm or coin inserted into it. The head of the household makes the sign of the cross over the cake three times with the knife, cuts it in four and then starts slicing it. The first slice goes to the Christ Child; the second to Saint Basil (*Ai Vassilis*), the Greek Santa Claus; the third to the poor; the next for any absent relatives. Only then does he portion out the pieces for himself and the family members present, in order of age. But you don't have to wait until the holidays to enjoy this.*

Ingredients *(Serves 8 to 12)*

* 3 cups/420 g all-purpose flour
* 1 tsp baking soda
* 16 tbsp/225 g unsalted butter
* 2 cups/400 g sugar
* 4 eggs, at room temperature
* 1 cup/150 g finely ground blanched almonds
* Grated zest of 1 lemon plus 1 tbsp lemon juice
* 1 cup/240 ml milk, scalded and cooled slightly
* ½ cup/120 ml brandy

1. Preheat the oven to 375°F/190°C. Butter a 9-inch/23-cm round cake pan and set aside.

2. Sift together the flour and baking soda. In the bowl of an electric mixer, cream the butter, add the sugar slowly, and beat until the mixture is light and fluffy. Add the eggs one at a time, beating until each egg is completely absorbed. Stir in the ground almonds and the lemon zest and juice. Then beat in the flour and the milk alternately, a little at a time. When you have finished the milk, start trickling in the brandy.

3. Scrape the batter into the prepared cake pan and bake until a knife inserted in the center comes out clean, 40 minutes to 1 hour. Let cool, turn out onto a plate, and serve.

ROBERT McCABE

Robert McCabe was born in Chicago in 1934 and grew up in the New York area. His fascination with photography began at the age of five with the gift of a Kodak Baby Brownie. While still an undergraduate at Princeton, he took his first photographs of France, Italy, and Greece during a trip in 1954. He returned to Greece in 1955 and 1957 and traveled extensively in the Aegean, shooting with a Rolleiflex and Plus-X film.

His black-and-white photos were first exhibited in 1954 and 1955 at Princeton. In 1967, a selection of his photographs was exhibited in New York under the auspices of Spyros Skouras. His first book, Metamorphosis, *was published in 1979.*

In recent years his images have been displayed at places as far flung as Wyoming, New York, London, Paris, and galleries all over Greece. His bestselling book, Greece: Images of an Enchanted Land 1954–1965, *was published in the United States and Greece. It is in its fourth printing. His photos of Greece have also appeared in numerous books by other authors.*

In addition to his work in Greece, McCabe has published books on Havana, Europe, North America, and Antarctica. Deep Freeze! A Photographer's Antarctic Odyssey in the Year 1959 *was issued in 2010 to commemorate the 100th anniversary of the attainment of the South Pole.* The Ramble in Central Park: A Wilderness West of Fifth *won a* Foreword Reviews *2011 Book of the Year award in the nature category.*

Meanwhile, several exhibitions are being planned on such subjects as Aegean island life in the 1950s, the Greeks and their seas, views of ruins with a twist from the 1950s, portraits of the Greeks, and traditional boats of the Aegean, while 2014 and 2016 saw the publication of the Greek and English editions of Mycenae.

WHAT IS YOUR FAVORITE GREEK FOOD?

Limnos dried figs à la Olga, as served by our friend AVL. *Horiatiki* salad with real old-fashioned tomatoes from the Peloponnese with capers and extra oregano. Santorini *fava* with onions and olive oil.

IN A FEW WORDS, WHAT DOES GREECE MEAN TO YOU?

More than 60 years ago I arrived in Greece for what was supposed to have been a 10-day visit. For reasons I still don't understand I felt immediately at home in the streets of Athens and in the islands and mountain villages. So 10 days has turned into 60 years, all very quickly. The changes witnessed have been enormous. It has been sad to watch the individual cultures of each Greek island disappear. But that's a very long story.

WHAT IS YOUR FONDEST MEMORY OF GREECE?

Wonderful memories of springtime in the Greek islands with balmy temperatures and wildflowers and a beautiful benign sea—but they can still be re-created today. So instead of trying to relive a memory, better to find the time to visit the Greek seas in springtime before the tourists arrive. It's just too bad that the old footpaths have been destroyed on so many islands. Patmos once had the most beautiful walk in the world, from Kampos to the beach of Livadi tou Yeranou, a stone path along a steep hillside above a magnificent coastline. For thousands of years it must have served as the main path to the north end of the island. A few years ago a bulldozer in one day completely destroyed three millennia of patinated beauty.

Puree of Split Yellow Peas with Toppings

Φάβα παντρεμένη · *Fava pandremeni*

Greek fava *is a puree of the yellow split pea,* Lathyrus clymenum *L., a member of the vetch family that is native to the volcanic island of Santorini. It should not be confused with the more common Italian word for the broad bean. Though the peas are grown in other parts of Greece, the dry conditions and soil minerals in Santorini produce peas with so much more flavor that a bag of them will cost three times more than other varieties you'll find at the grocer's. They are worth it, though. Fava is a favorite taverna staple. There it's usually served sprinkled with finely sliced raw onions and olive oil, with slices of lemon. For a more elegant presentation, serve it with caramelized onions, capers, and chopped sun-dried tomatoes. Accompany this dish with a loaf of fresh bread.*

Ingredients

(Serves 4 to 6 as an appetizer)

* 8 oz/225 g yellow split peas, preferably from Santorini, picked over and rinsed
* 6 cups/1.4 l cold water
* Salt and freshly ground black pepper
* 1 onion, peeled and left whole, plus 2 onions, sliced
* ⅓ cup/75 ml extra-virgin olive oil, plus extra for frying
* 3 tbsp lemon juice
* Capers
* Sun-dried tomatoes, chopped

1 Place the peas and the water in a large saucepan, season with salt and pepper, and bring to a boil. Reduce the heat and simmer, skimming off the foam as necessary, for about 10 minutes. Add the whole onion and simmer until the peas are soft and have begun to disintegrate, 40 to 50 minutes. Stir occasionally to keep the peas from sticking to the bottom of the pot, and add more water if necessary.

2 While the split peas are cooking, pour a few tablespoons of oil into a large skillet and heat over medium-low heat. Add the sliced onions and fry slowly, stirring occasionally, until golden brown and caramelized. Let them drain on a paper towel–lined plate, then transfer to a bowl. Put the capers and sun-dried tomatoes in separate bowls.

3 Remove the onion from the split peas and discard. Pour in the oil, lemon juice, and more salt and pepper, while stirring vigorously with a wooden spoon, until you have a puree. (To make a smoother puree, you can either use a blender or a hand blender.) Transfer the puree to a serving bowl and serve with the onions, capers, and tomatoes.

SOFKA ZINOVIEFF

Sofka is a writer and journalist who has written extensively about Greece. She was born in London, and her father's parents were refugees from the Russian revolution. She studied social anthropology at Cambridge and first lived in Greece in the late 1980s while doing research for her doctoral degree. She and her Greek husband lived in Moscow, London, and Rome before settling in Athens in 2001 with their two daughters. Her books include Eurydice Street: A Place in Athens, *a memoir in search of the meaning of being Greek;* Red Princess: A Revolutionary Life, *a biography of her flamboyant, leftist grandmother;* The House on Paradise Street, *a novel about a family in contemporary Athens and their troubled history during the Greek civil war; and her latest,* The Mad Boy, Lord Berners, My Grandmother and Me, *a biography about the eccentrics in her family.*

WHAT IS YOUR FAVORITE GREEK FOOD?

"Married sardines"—grilled fillets of sardine that have been paired with a secret package of garlic and herbs binding them together. Greece has amazing and varied dishes but its raw ingredients offer such wonderful tastes that the best food is sometimes the simplest—it's hard to beat just-caught grilled fish, a colorful salad of whatever's in season with plenty of herbs and olives and the best olive oil, and fresh-baked bread.

IN A FEW WORDS, WHAT DOES GREECE MEAN TO YOU?

Greece is the country I embraced as a student, that I adopted as my home, where I brought up my children, that I have written about in my books, and where I feel happiest in the world.

WHAT IS YOUR FONDEST MEMORY OF GREECE?

Arriving at my favorite island by boat at 3 a.m. and taking the dark, coastal road that smells of Greek summer nights—warm pine, jasmine, fig leaves, and the sea. The memory only gets fonder each time I return, layering the minor variations in pleasure as the experience is repeated.

Eggplant "Little Shoes" with Vegetable Filling

Παπουτσάκια · Papoutsakia

Eggplants are my favorite Greek vegetable and the number of dishes using them is endless. These "little shoes" look like their name, as the eggplant is cut lengthwise, stuffed, and covered with béchamel.

1 *For the béchamel sauce:* Melt the butter in a medium saucepan over medium heat, stir in the flour, and cook for 1 to 2 minutes, stirring. Off the heat, gradually whisk in the warm milk, return to a simmer and stir until you have a smooth sauce. Season with salt and pepper to taste.

2 Preheat the oven to 350°F/180°C.

3 Scoop the flesh out of the eggplant halves, leaving a shell. Chop the eggplant flesh. Heat the oil in a large frying pan, add the onions, and cook until soft. Add the chopped eggplant flesh, celery, garlic, and paprika, salt, and pepper to taste and toss them in the oil. Add the tomatoes and simmer for 15 minutes.

4 Mix in the feta and parsley and stuff the eggplant shells. Place them in a baking dish and cover with a thin layer of béchamel sauce. Bake until golden brown on top, about 30 minutes, then serve.

Ingredients *(Serves 4)*

Béchamel Sauce:

* 4 tbsp/60 g unsalted butter
* ⅓ cup/60 g all-purpose flour
* 2½ cups/600 ml milk, warmed
* Salt and freshly ground black pepper

* 4 medium eggplants, halved lengthwise
* ¼ cup/60 ml olive oil
* 4 onions, chopped
* 3 celery stalks, chopped
* 6 garlic cloves, chopped
* Paprika
* Salt and freshly ground black pepper
* 5 tomatoes, chopped
* 8 oz/250 g feta cheese, crumbled (2 cups)
* Chopped fresh parsley

i

You can make a meaty version by sautéing 8 ounces/250 g ground beef or lamb with the onions. For a lighter version, instead of covering the eggplant with the béchamel, you can sprinkle a hard cheese like kefalotyri *or* graviera *over them and then top with breadcrumbs.*

"Married Sardines"

Σαρδέλες παντρεμένες · *Sardeles pandremenes*

Paired-up fillets of fresh sardines made into little packages with a herby, garlic center.

1 *For the sardines and filling:* Light a gas or charcoal grill. Mix the parsley and garlic together and add the oil, lemon juice, oregano, and salt to taste.
Open the fish fillets on a plate. Spread a teaspoon of filling on both halves.
Take another filleted fish and place it on top of the first, to enclose the filling.
Repeat until you have "married" all the fillets.
Drizzle a little oil on top of them and place them on the grill. Cook for 5 to 7 minutes to a side, depending on the size of the sardines.

2 *For the salsa:* Combine the tomatoes, onion, capers, cilantro (if using), and jalapeño in a bowl. Drizzle with some olive oil, season with salt and pepper to taste, and stir.

3 Place the married sardine couples around the edge of a circular plate with a mound of the salsa in the middle. Serve.

i *Instead of grilling the sardines, you can cook them under a broiler, or in a very hot oven for about 15 minutes.*

Ingredients *(Serves 4 to 6 as an appetizer)*

Sardines and Filling

* 2 cups/200 g chopped fresh parsley
* 4 garlic cloves, finely chopped
* ¼ cup/60 ml extra-virgin olive oil, plus extra for drizzling
* Juice of 1 lemon
* 1 tsp dried oregano
* Salt
* 24 fresh sardines, cleaned and filleted

Salsa

* 2 tomatoes, peeled and finely chopped
* 1 onion, finely chopped
* ¼ cup/35 g capers
* Handful chopped fresh cilantro (optional)
* 1 jalapeño chile, stemmed, seeded, and minced
* Extra-virgin olive oil
* Salt and freshly ground black pepper

Pavlos's Secret Chickpea Stew

Η μυστική ρεβιθάδα του Παύλου · *I mystiki revithada tou Pavlou*

It took about 10 years of eating these delectable chickpeas at Flisvos Taverna on Patmos before I was told the secret recipe of this rich, aromatic dish that features rosemary, white wine, and plenty of onions.

Ingredients *(Serves 8 to 10)*

* 1 lb/500 g dried chickpeas, soaked overnight and drained
* 4 onions, peeled
* ¼ cup/60 ml extra-virgin olive oil
* 1 cup/240 ml white wine
* 2 tbsp finely chopped fresh rosemary
* Salt and freshly ground black pepper

1. Place the chickpeas in a large pot, cover them with plenty of fresh water, add 2 whole onions, and bring to a boil, removing the foam. Simmer over medium heat for 45 minutes, then drain the chickpeas in a colander, reserving the cooking liquid and the onions.

2. While the chickpeas cook, chop the 2 uncooked onions. Heat the oil in a large skillet over medium heat, add the chopped onions, and cook until soft and translucent.

3. Preheat the oven to 325°F/170°C.

4. Puree one-third of the chickpeas with the 2 boiled onions and some of the cooking liquid. Transfer to an ovenproof earthenware pot or a Dutch oven and add the remaining chickpeas, the fried onions and their oil, the wine, rosemary, and salt and pepper to taste. Cook for at least 2 hours—even longer is fine. You may need to add some of the reserved liquid. A nice crust forms, making this thick stew dish even more delectable. Serve.

SOPHIA VARI

Sophia Vari is a Greek artist who lives and works in Monaco. Born in Athens to a Greek father and a Hungarian mother, Sophia spent part of her childhood in Switzerland, studied in England and France, and currently divides her time between New York, Monaco, and Pietrasanta, Italy. Famous for both her painting and sculpture, she has exhibited her work in Paris, Athens, Florence, Baden Baden, New York, and Caracas. Her work is strongly influenced by Mayan, Egyptian, Olmec, and Cycladic traditions as well as Ancient and Baroque aesthetics. She is married to the well-known Colombian painter Fernando Botero.

WHAT IS YOUR FAVORITE GREEK FOOD?

My favorite food in Greece is *tiropites* (cheese pies). You can eat them at any time and find them anywhere and everywhere. But I also love *dolmades*, stuffed with rice, made with fresh grape leaves that you've picked yourself from the vine.

IN A FEW WORDS, WHAT DOES GREECE MEAN TO YOU?

Your country, you have it in your blood, in your soul, in your taste . . . Your love for it is pure and no matter where you go, however beautiful, exciting, and admirable the place might be, it will never be like your country, especially when that country is Greece.

WHAT IS YOUR FONDEST MEMORY OF GREECE?

My fondest memory of Greece is the fragrance of jasmine.

Cretan Cheese Pies

Καλιτσούνια · *Kalitsounia*

The filling used is encountered from one end of Crete to the other, in towns and in villages. Cheese and mint seems to be a favorite Cretan marriage of tastes, the tangy mint giving the mild cheese a refreshing zip. But if you'd rather have a hot than a cool effect, do as the Jews of Chania once did and add one or two finely chopped chile peppers to the cheese instead of mint. This pastry freezes well.

Ingredients

(Makes about 2 dozen small half-moon pies)

- 2½ cups/350 g bread flour
- ½ tsp salt
- 3 tbsp olive oil
- About ¾ cup/180 ml warm water
- 8 oz/225 g *myzithra* cheese or a combination of cream cheese and ricotta
- 1½ tbsp chopped fresh mint
- Light vegetable oil for frying

1 Place the flour on a clean counter. Make a well in the center and add the salt and olive oil. Then swirl in the water, little by little, mixing with your fingers until you have a medium-soft dough. Knead it with the heel of your hand for about 5 minutes, punching, rotating and pushing in the sides until it is smooth and malleable. Cover with plastic wrap and set aside to rest in a cool place for at least 30 minutes. (It will keep in the refrigerator for up to 3 days.)

2 Drain the cheese on several layers of paper towels if it is very loose and watery. Transfer to a bowl, add the mint, and use with a fork to mash the cheese and mint together until the cheese is smooth and well blended.

3 Separate the dough into 2 or 3 balls and roll out on a lightly floured counter until it is no more than ⅜ inch/1 cm thick. Using a teacup or cookie cutter, cut the dough into circles. Put a teaspoonful of filling in the center of each circle and fold 1 side over into a half-moon. Press the edges together to seal (a tiny bit of water on your finger will help). Repeat until you have used up all the pastry.

4 Heat 4 or 5 inches of oil in a large saucepan to 375°F/190°C. Working in batches, fry the *tiropites* on both sides until light golden brown. Drain on paper towels and serve.

Grape Leaves Stuffed with Rice

Ντολμαδάκια γιαλαντζί με ρύζι · Dolmadakia yialantzi me rizi

These perennial favorites were initially prepared as a fasting dish and therefore had no meat. The word yialantzi *used to describe them actually means "fake" or "counterfeit" in Turkish, but there's nothing fake about their taste. The word* dolmadakia *also has Turkish roots, from* dolma, *"to stuff." These are equally good hot or cold.*

1 Heat 5 tablespoons of the oil in a large saucepan over medium heat and brown the pine nuts lightly. Add the green onions and white onion and cook, stirring, until they become shiny and translucent.
Add the rice to the pan and cook, stirring, until the rice is opaque, 2 to 3 minutes.
Add the hot water and season with salt and pepper to taste. Lower the heat and simmer until the rice has absorbed all the liquid.
Transfer the rice to a bowl, stir in the chopped dill, mint, and parsley, and set aside to cool.

2 Bring a pot of water to a boil, add the grape leaves, and cook for 5 minutes to soften them. Plunge them into cold water and drain them in a colander. Line the bottom of the saucepan (you can use the one you cooked the rice in) with a few grape leaves.
Any torn ones will be fine for this purpose.

3 To fill the rest, place each leaf vein-side up with the base facing you on a flat surface.
Put a spoonful of filling near the bottom, fold over the 2 sides and roll up to the top. Repeat until you have finished with the leaves and the filling.

Ingredients *(Makes about 30 pieces)*

- ½ cup/120 ml olive oil
- 2 tbsp pine nuts, finely chopped
- 2 cups/200 g green onions, white part only, finely chopped
- 1 white onion, finely chopped
- 1 cup/200 g long-grain white rice, rinsed
- 1 cup/240 ml water or vegetable broth, hot, plus extra for cooking the *dolmadakia*
- Salt and freshly ground black pepper
- ½ bunch fresh dill, finely chopped
- ½ bunch fresh mint, finely chopped
- ¼ bunch fresh parsley, finely chopped
- 1 (14- to 16-oz/400- to 455-g) jar grape leaves in brine or 35 fresh grape leaves
- Juice of 1 large lemon, plus lemon slices for serving
- Greek yogurt

4 Place the *dolmadakia* carefully in the pan, seam-side down and close to each other to keep them from unrolling. Add the remaining 3 tablespoons oil and the lemon juice, season with salt, and add water or broth to cover the bundles. Finally, place any spare leaves over the top and cover them with a plate that will just fit in the pan. (This will keep them from moving and breaking during cooking.) Simmer over low heat for about 45 minutes, adding a little liquid if necessary.
Serve hot or cold with slices of lemon and thick Greek yogurt.

If you're going to serve these dolmadakia *cold, let them cool in their own juices and covered with the plate to preserve their green color.* *i*

PRINCESS TATIANA

Princess Tatiana (née Tatiana Blatnik) was born in Caracas, Venezuela. After graduating from Aiglon College in Switzerland, she received her B.A. in sociology from Georgetown University in 2003. In 2006 she joined Diane von Furstenberg's fashion house as public relations consultant and event organizer.

In 2010 she married Prince Nikolaos on the island of Spetses. Since then and especially after moving to Athens in 2013, Tatiana has actively pursued her passion for natural and healthy living through her philanthropic and entrepreneurial work. She cofounded Elpida Youth, which aims to raise awareness about and support the psychological well-being of sick children. She has also joined forces with the local nonprofit organization Boroume. Tatiana recently cofounded TRIA, a company that collaborates with local artisans and artistic minds to create products of unique and high-quality craftsmanship, celebrating Greece's heritage and new talent.

Tatiana has worked with numerous charities in the past, including the Red Cross (Royal Patron, 2011); Vital Voices, in support of emerging women leaders around the world; and the JuanFe Foundation, which aims to improve the quality of life of impoverished children and teenage mothers in the city of Cartagena, Colombia. She is a board member of the Walkabout Foundation and a Young Patron of the Museum of Cycladic Art in Athens, Greece.

WHAT IS YOUR FAVORITE GREEK FOOD?

This is a very, very difficult one for me . . . Where do I start? I love the tastes of the simplest, purest ingredients: cucumbers are sweet; walnuts are not bitter and they melt in your mouth; olive oil is my liquid gold that I pour on almost everything, its taste and nutritional benefits outweighing all I have ever tried; oregano lifts any salad; the combination of tahini, honey, and cinnamon with the crispest, juiciest apples from the area around Volos in Central Greece is what I jump out of bed for in the mornings. I love all healthy fruits, greens, and charcoal-grilled fish but, I have to admit, my absolute favorite indulgences have to be dishes with the amazing cornucopia of Greek cheeses. The list is endless but for me, so far, there is nothing better than a plate of hot, melted *saganaki* (fried cheese) or *dakos* salad from the island of Crete, a delicious combination of *paximadi* (rye rusks) topped with chopped tomatoes, crumbled feta, oregano, and, of course, olive oil. (Fun fact: To soften and season the rusks, villagers would soak them in sea water and then add the rest of the ingredients.) Finally, there is grilled *halloumi* (a type of chewy cheese originally from Cyprus), which I use in my "Paxos salad" named after the idyllic island on which I first had it, Paxos.

IN A FEW WORDS, WHAT DOES GREECE MEAN TO YOU?

Simply put, Greece is a country I love and now call home. Since moving here in 2013, I find there are two words that best describe Greece in my mind: antithesis and plethora. Greece is the loudest but also one of the most serene places I have ever been to; it has the brightest as well as the stormiest skies; the richest and, at the same time, simplest flavors I have ever tasted—to name a few contrasts. And, of course, such a great abundance of history, knowledge, and tradition . . . In fact, I think it is exactly that—Greece's extremes and nontangible wealth—that makes her charming to both locals and visitors. This is the beauty and captivating mystery that seemed a bit foreign and incomprehensible to me at first but that, now having opened myself to it, feels familiar and even irresistible.

WHAT IS YOUR FONDEST MEMORY OF GREECE?

Most of my memories of Greece are very emotional. The two that that stand out most are visiting for the first time with my husband back in 2003, and getting married on the island of Spetses seven years later. I will never forget the intensity of Nikolaos's emotions when reunited with his home country in 2003. We watched every single sunset and sunrise for the first few days that we spent in Greece—in fact, it was one of the most powerful experiences that we have ever shared. Our wedding day in the summer of 2010 was another moment that will be forever engraved in my memory. Ever since then, as I "come into harbors seen for the first time," as the poet Cavafy writes—be it a daily trip to the market for fresh seasonal produce, meeting people for the first time, or embarking on a new project—I am equally grateful for the adventure that awaits me every morning, constantly creating new memories.

My "Paxos" Salad

Σαλάτα από τους Παξούς · *Salata apo tous Paxous*

Paxos, a tiny, olive-covered island south of Corfu, is always referred to in the plural in Greek because it has an even smaller sister islet next door called Antipaxos. Both have white sand beaches and turquoise waters, and it is here that my husband and I enjoyed eating this salad, picnic-style, on a very small boat on which we made our first solo boat trip after getting our boating license in Corfu when we moved to Greece in 2013.

I Combine the oil, vinegar, lemon zest, and honey in a jam jar with a pinch of salt and pepper, cover, and shake well. Spread the arugula in a salad bowl or platter and arrange the remaining salad ingredients on top of it. Drizzle the dressing on top and serve at once.

i Halloumi *is a rubbery cheese from Cyprus that doesn't taste like much cold, but is absolutely wonderful on its own grilled or fried, with just a few drops of lemon juice to enhance it. If you can't find it, use provolone cheese and don't grill it.* Noumboulo, *a specialty of Corfu, is a cured pork fillet with a delicate, sweet flavor; prosciutto makes a good substitute.*

Ingredients *(Serves 4)*

- 10 tbsp/150 ml extra-virgin olive oil
- ¼ cup/60 ml balsamic vinegar
- Zest of ½ lemon
- ½ tsp honey
- Sea salt and freshly ground black pepper
- 4 oz/115 g baby arugula (4 cups)
- 8 oz/225 g *halloumi* cheese, sliced, grilled, and cut into thin strips
- 2 boneless, skinless chicken breasts (about 12 oz/340 g total), trimmed, grilled, and cut into thin strips
- 12 thin slices *noumboulo* or prosciutto
- 4–5 fresh figs, quartered
- 2 tbsp chopped walnuts

Fish en Papillote with Greek Aromas

Ψάρι ψημένο σε λαδόκολλα με Ελληνικά αρώματα
Psari psimeno se ladokolla me ellinika aromata

Many people are intimidated by fish and prefer to eat it in restaurants. Moving to Greece has allowed me to explore and enjoy cooking fish at home. I love making this dish because it is so simple and quick. The most wonderful part of this is opening up your little parcel of fish. It is a complete sensory experience; you feel and smell the aromatic steam that gently warms your skin while also enjoying the sight of the rainbow of colors and then, finally, the taste: Simple. Delicious. Fresh.

Ingredients *(Serves 4)*

* ¼ cup/60 ml olive oil
* Grated zest and juice of 1 lemon
* 12 cherry tomatoes, halved
* 12 black olives, pitted
* Salt and freshly ground black pepper
* 4 (6-oz/170-g) fish fillets, preferably gilt-head bream (*tsipoura*), sea bass, or snapper
* 4 sprigs rosemary

1 Preheat the oven to 350°/F180°C.

2 Combine the oil, lemon zest and juice, tomatoes, and olives in a medium bowl and season with salt and pepper to taste. Add the fish fillets and let marinate for 5 minutes. Cut 4 pieces of parchment paper or aluminum foil, 12 inches/30 cm square.

3 Place a fish fillet together with some of the marinade, tomatoes, and olives on 1 side of a sheet of paper and place a rosemary sprig on top. Fold the paper over the fish and crimp the edges tightly to make a rectangular envelope. (The idea is that some steam should remain inside.) Repeat with the remaining fillets, marinade, and rosemary to make 4 packets.

4 Place the packets on a baking sheet and cook for 12 minutes. Open carefully and serve.

i

I like to serve these with a large plate of grilled vegetables, a large green salad and a simple potato salad from Mani, which I learned about at an olive oil seminar. It couldn't be easier: Mash some warm boiled potatoes with a fork and add a few good splashes of olive oil, some sea salt, and fresh chopped parsley. Briam *(see p. 94) also goes very well.*

Sweet Potato Pancakes with Tahini, Honey & Cinnamon

Γλυκοπατάτες τηγανιτές με ταχίνι, μέλι, και κανέλα
Glykopatates tiganites me tahini, meli, kai kanella

This is my favorite breakfast; the combination of ingredients keeps me going for hours. I discovered tahini when I moved to Greece. I never used to eat it and now I eat it for breakfast, as a snack with fruits, and in salad dressing. I love Fuji apples from Volos in Greece, but you can just use your favorite apple variety.

1 Combine the sweet potato and apple in a bowl. Add the egg whites (or use whole eggs if you prefer to make more of a sweet potato scramble), currants (if using), flax seeds (if using), cinnamon, and salt. Beat everything together with a fork.

2 Heat the oil in a large skillet over medium-low heat. Form the mixture into 2 or 3 round patties and place them in the skillet. Cook 2 to 3 minutes, or until brown, flip, and cook an additional 1 to 2 minutes. Top with a generous serving of tahini, honey, and cinnamon. Breakfast is served!

i *Greece has the most incredible honey varieties; I love thyme and pine the most. I am blessed in Greece as I have the opportunity to meet local honey producers—I suggest you try and source out your own in your local community as well.*

Ingredients *(Makes 2 to 3 pancakes)*

* 1 small sweet potato, peeled and grated
* ½ apple, coarsely chopped
* 2 egg whites or 2 whole eggs
* Handful currants (optional)
* 1 tbsp ground flax seeds or almond flour (optional)
* ½ tsp ground cinnamon, plus extra for sprinkling
* ¼ tsp sea salt
* 1 tsp extra-virgin olive oil or coconut oil
* Honey, preferably wildflower
* Tahini (lots of it)

TATIANA CASIRAGHI

Tatiana Casiraghi (née Santo Domingo) is married to Andrea Casiraghi, the eldest son of the Princess of Hanover and grandson of Prince Rainier and Grace Kelly. In 2011, she launched, with Dana Alikhani, Muzungu Sisters, a fashion brand of ethically sourced, handmade luxury clothes produced by artisans around the world celebrated for their skill. Tatiana and her husband support several charity organizations, most notably the Motrice Foundation, which funds research into cerebral palsy. With a Colombian father and Brazilian mother, Tatiana, who was born in New York and brought up in Switzerland, speaks four languages fluently.

WHAT IS YOUR FAVORITE GREEK FOOD?

My favorite Greek dish is *strapatsada* (scrambled eggs with tomatoes)—it's easy to make and delicious. I often make it and am happy to have it at any meal of the day.

IN A FEW WORDS, WHAT DOES GREECE MEAN TO YOU?

Greece is the perfect combination of an easygoing and relaxed atmosphere, crystal clear beautiful waters, and delicious food—the ideal holiday destination.

WHAT IS YOUR FONDEST MEMORY OF GREECE?

My fondest memory of Greece is of late lunches at Kiki's Taverna in Agios Sostis beach on Mykonos. I love that beach, and Kiki's is one of my favorite restaurants in the world. A truly magical spot.

Scrambled Eggs with Tomatoes

Στραπατσάδα · Strapatsada

You won't find this dish in any taverna, but this is comfort food at its best and simplest, every child's favorite and a favorite with children of any age, especially when the eggs are accompanied by fried potatoes right out of the pan.

Ingredients *(Serves 4 or 5)*

* ¼ cup/60 ml extra-virgin olive oil
* 4 large tomatoes, chopped
* Salt and freshly ground black pepper
* Pinch sugar (optional)
* 8 eggs, beaten

I Heat the oil in a large skillet over medium heat, add the tomatoes, season with salt, pepper, and sugar (if using), and simmer until the oil and the tomatoes separate. Lower the heat, stir in the eggs, and cook gently until the eggs are cooked and any juice from the tomatoes has evaporated. Serve hot.

i *If you can be bothered, cut the tomatoes in half, seed them, grate them, and discard the skins—the result will be more refined. The pinch of sugar brings out the flavor of tomatoes but depending on the quality of your tomatoes, it may not be needed.*

VALENTINO & GIANCARLO GIAMMETTI

WHAT IS YOUR FAVORITE GREEK FOOD?

Any dish that includes feta.

IN A FEW WORDS, WHAT DOES GREECE MEAN TO YOU?

To us, Greece means fun, freedom, and relaxation.

WHAT IS YOUR FONDEST MEMORY OF GREECE?

The 2004 Olympic Games in Athens.

Mousse de Feta à la Grecque

Μους με φέτα · Mousse me feta

Accompany this savory mousse with cherry tomatoes and torn basil leaves, a green salad, a selection of grilled vegetables, baked figs, olives, crackers, or anything else you fancy.

Ingredients *(Serves 8 to 10)*

- 3½ tsp powdered gelatin
- 1¼ cups/300 ml heavy cream
- 10 oz/300 g feta cheese
- 5 oz/150 g fresh goat cheese
- ⅓ cup/60 g black olives, pitted and coarsely chopped
- Salt (optional)

1 Sprinkle the gelatin over ¼ cup/60 ml of the cream in a small bowl and set it aside for 5 minutes to soften. Heat the gelatin-cream mixture in a microwave until the cream is bubbling and the gelatin is dissolved, about 30 seconds; let cool slightly. Grate the feta into a large bowl, add the goat cheese, and mix thoroughly. Add the gelatin-cream mixture to the cheeses and whisk together, then stir in the chopped olives.

2 Whip the remaining 1 cup/240 ml cream with an electric mixer until it is thick but not too stiff, then gently fold it into the cheese mixture, taking care not to stir too much so the cream remains fluffy and light. Season with salt to taste. (The feta and olives being salty, you may not need to add any salt.)

3 Scrape the mousse into a 3-cup metal mold and refrigerate until set, about 2 hours. To unmold the mousse, heat the edges of the mold with a blowtorch or dip for a few seconds in hot water and slide it onto a platter.

VICKY VLACHONIS

Vicky Vlachonis was born in Athens, Greece, to a tennis coach father and a yoga teacher/health guru mother, who taught her to be active and understand the importance of food and meditation. She began her professional career in England as an osteopath and musculoskeletal specialist treating dancers from London's Royal Ballet and major productions such as Cats *and* The Lion King*. After working in London's most prestigious holistic clinics, she established her own practice in 2001. Today, Vicky shares her holistic healing treatments and methods all around the world, helping clients release their pain and get radiant before PTA meetings and play dates, concerts and board meetings, movie shoots and red carpet events. She has treated such notable personalities as Gwyneth Paltrow, Cameron Diaz, Elton John, and Katy Perry. She lives with her family and practices in Beverly Hills, California.*

WHAT IS YOUR FAVORITE GREEK FOOD?

Greek extra-virgin olive oil is one of my favorite Greek foods. I wake up each morning and have four tablespoonfuls of olive oil for its pain-fighting benefits. In Greece, olive oil is a staple at almost every meal. I also love organic Greek yogurt and healing tea made from Greek oregano.

IN A FEW WORDS, WHAT DOES GREECE MEAN TO YOU?

Greece is my home, where my heart and soul belong. When I land in Greece, I feel grounded. Greece means love, family, healing foods, beautiful islands, childhood memories, prayer, being mindful, and giving back.

WHAT IS YOUR FONDEST MEMORY OF GREECE?

My fondest memory of Greece is spending hours at the dining table with my family and loved ones. We'd eat, drink, laugh, dance, sing, cry, shout, and talk about everything. This is where we'd analyze our dreams, emotions, thoughts, and feelings about the past, present, and future. I especially love the naps after a long lunch. The dining table is where my family would come together to enjoy my mum's delicious food and spend quality time with one another.

Scientists believe that **olive oil** (especially extra virgin) is really the key component of the super-healthy Mediterranean diet. Extra-virgin olive oil contains natural alcohol-like chemicals called phenolic compounds that have various anti-inflammatory powers, the strongest of which is oleocanthal. Oleocanthal is like natural ibuprofen—it has the same molecular profile and prostagladin-blocking function. Four tablespoons of extra virgin olive oil provides the same effect as taking 1/10 of an adult dose of ibuprofen. This is not to say that your salad's dressing is going to cure your back pain, but researchers believe eating some olive oil every day—as I've done since childhood—blocks the prostaglandin cascade, tamping down inflammation on a regular basis, which may prevent diseases like Alzheimer's and be especially helpful for managing chronic pain. You'll know your extra-virgin olive oil has a high dose of oleocanthal if it has a strong peppery or spicy taste and creates a slight tingling sensation in your throat. Look for organic olive oil that is fresh from the press and has a "vintage" harvest date. Unlike wine, it does not improve with age, and the shelf life of commercial oils is no more than a year.

Peas & Artichoke Hearts

Αγγινάρες με αρακά · Anginares me araka

1 Place the peas, artichoke hearts, yellow onions, green onions, carrots, and dill in a large saucepan. Add the broth, cover, and simmer for 30 minutes.

2 Remove the pan from the heat and add the oil and lemon juice, along with salt and pepper to taste. Let the dish rest for 15 minutes and serve.

Ingredients *(Serves 4 to 5)*

- 2 cups/280 g shelled fresh or frozen peas
- 10 canned or frozen organic artichoke hearts
- 1 cup/160 g chopped yellow onions
- ½ cup/50 g thinly sliced green onions
- 2 carrots, peeled and cut in large chunks
- ½ cup/30 g finely chopped fresh dill
- 1 cup/240 ml vegetable broth
- 2–3 tbsp extra-virgin olive oil
- Juice of ½ lemon
- Sea salt and freshly ground black pepper

Beans with Tomato Sauce

Φασολάκια λαδερά · *Fasolakia ladera*

Adding the olive oil after cooking makes food more digestible and healthier.

1 Place the green beans, onions, and parsley in a large pot. Add the tomato puree, broth, and cinnamon stick. Bring to a boil over medium heat, then reduce the heat to low and simmer uncovered for 45 minutes, until the vegetables are tender and most of the liquid has been absorbed.

2 Remove the pot from the heat and stir in the oil. Let the dish rest for 15 minutes and serve.

Ingredients *(Serves 4 to 6)*

- 2 lb/1 kg thin green beans, trimmed and cut in half
- 2 large yellow onions, thinly sliced
- 1 cup/60 g finely chopped fresh parsley
- 3 cups/750 g tomatoes, pureed in a blender
- 2 cups/480 ml vegetable broth
- 1 large cinnamon stick
- 3–4 tbsp extra-virgin olive oil

Goat with Prunes

Κατσικάκι στη γάστρα με δαμάσκηνα · *Katsikaki sti gastra me damaskina*

This dish is delicious on its own or accompanied with brown rice, quinoa, or pearl barley.

1 Place the meat, onions, prunes, lemon juice, broth, garlic, and oregano in a large pot or Dutch oven and season with salt and pepper.

2 Bring to a boil, turn down the heat to medium-low, cover, and cook until the meat and vegetables are tender and the liquid has been reduced by about half, 1½ to 2 hours. (Give the meat a stir about halfway through.)

3 Transfer the meat and vegetables to a platter and drizzle with the oil to give the meat a nice sheen. Serve.

Ingredients *(Serves 4)*

* 2 good-sized goat or lamb thighs, trimmed and cut into 3-inch/7.5 cm pieces
* 3 white or yellow onions, sliced
* 2 cups/350 g pitted prunes
* 1 cup/240 ml freshly squeezed lemon juice (about 5 lemons)
* 1 cup/240 ml vegetable broth
* 1 tbsp finely chopped garlic
* 1 tbsp dried oregano
* Sea salt and freshly ground black pepper
* ½ cup/120 ml extra-virgin olive oil

Most of us know **oregano** from the spice cabinet—but I keep mine in the teapot! Steeping oregano leaves in or adding a few drops of oregano essential oil to hot water allows me to enjoy a relaxing, soothing anti-inflammatory treat that increases my intake of two of oregano's strongest antimicrobial compounds, thymol and carvacrol, which have been clinically proven to kill antibacterial resistant strains of Staphylococcus aureus (including strains of the dreaded MRSA). Oregano is more effective than pharmaceuticals because it can penetrate the biofilm that protects these nasty bugs and makes them so strong. Packed with antioxidants, oregano also protects the liver, fights tumor formation, and kills parasites in the gut, all of which can soothe or prevent pain-causing inflammation.

VICTORIA HISLOP

*Novelist Victoria Hislop studied English literature at Oxford University. In 2005, her first book (*The Island*, about Spinalonga, the abandoned leper colony on Crete) became an international bestseller. With over three million copies sold worldwide, it was turned into a 26-part Greek TV series. She was named Newcomer of the Year at the British Book Awards and is now an ambassador for the international charity Lepra. Since then, apart from a novel about the Spanish Civil War, she has focused her attention on Greek subjects: 20th-century Thessaloniki in* The Thread; The Last Dance and Other Stories, *set in Greece; and* The Sunrise, *set in Cyprus, a number one bestseller in England and in Greece. Victoria's books have been translated into more than 35 languages. She has won several literary awards in France. She divides her time between the UK and Greece.*

WHAT IS YOUR FAVORITE GREEK FOOD?

I am a vegetarian, so Greece offers me a huge variety, especially in Crete. I adore *horta* (Greek greens), *fava* (yellow split pea puree), zucchini (fried, or made into fritters, or zucchini blossoms stuffed with rice), wonderful cheese, and so on. With all these things on offer, I can't see why anyone needs meat. If I had to name one thing that I could actually live on, it would be *fava* (see p. 156). I adore it. Every time I eat it in a restaurant or when I make it myself, it tastes a bit different, but always very wholesome and healthy and filling.

IN A FEW WORDS, WHAT DOES GREECE MEAN TO YOU?

Greece means a million things to me. Where to begin? A landscape, a culture, a cuisine, a language, and a climate that I love. They just seem to suit me; they put me in a good mood, like the translucent light that seems to illuminate this country. Perhaps most important of all, though, are the people. I enjoy meeting people here so much and will never tire of trying to understand the Greek mentality. Every person I meet teaches me something.

WHAT IS YOUR FONDEST MEMORY OF GREECE?

I have so many, it's almost impossible to name just one. But a unique one was this: We had just finished all the filming for the TV serial of *To Nisi* (*The Island*), and a crowd gathered to celebrate in the village of Plaka opposite Spinalonga. The production had involved literally hundreds of people (actors, extras, crew, technicians) and it was January. There was a huge *vassilopita* (New Year's Cake), which was cut and shared, there was singing and dancing, which I always find very hypnotic in Crete. It had a surreal quality to it. But I think it happened.

Zucchini Fritters with Tzatziki

Κολοκυθοκεφτέδες & Τζατζίκι · *Kolokythokeftedes & Tzatziki*

One of Greece's best-loved mezedes, *this dip goes especially well with fried eggplant, zucchini slices, or beet salad, but it is also an indispensable ingredient in a pita with souvlaki or gyro. It can be as garlicky as you want, while the mint and cucumber make it cool and refreshing. It's important to use the best Greek yogurt you can find for this dip.*

1 *For the tzatziki:* Squeeze out as much liquid as you can from the cucumber and then mix all the ingredients together. Season to taste and refrigerate for several hours so that the flavors blend before serving.

2 Bring a large pot of water to a boil, add the zucchini, and cook for about 3 minutes from the time the water returns to a rollicking boil. Drain, and when cool enough to handle, squeeze all the water out of the zucchini. Transfer the zucchini to a large bowl and add the breadcrumbs, onion, eggs, parsley, mint, feta, flour, oil, and salt and pepper to taste. Mix thoroughly and refrigerate for at least an hour before cooking.

3 When you're ready to eat shape the fritters into slightly flattened little balls by rolling a tablespoonful of the mixture between your palms, and then dredge them in flour—either on a plate or by shaking them gently, a few at a time, in a paper bag with a few tablespoons of flour in it. Heat 1 inch/2.5 cm of oil in a large skillet until it is hot but not smoking and, working in batches (don't overcrowd), fry the balls until they are browned on both sides. Drain them on paper towels and serve with the tzaziki.

Ingredients *(Makes about 30 fritters)*

Tzatziki

- ½ long cucumber, peeled and grated (about 1 cup/140 g)
- 2 cups/550 g Greek yogurt
- 1 tbsp chopped fresh mint
- 2–3 garlic cloves, minced
- 1 tbsp extra-virgin olive oil
- Salt and freshly ground black pepper

- 2 lb/1 kg zucchini, grated
- 1 cup/110 g dry breadcrumbs
- 1 onion, grated
- 2 eggs, beaten
- 1–2 handfuls chopped fresh parsley
- 1–2 handfuls chopped fresh mint
- 1 oz/30 g crumbled soft feta cheese, or to taste
- 2 tbsp all-purpose flour, plus extra for dredging
- 2 tbsp olive oil, plus extra for frying
- Salt and freshly ground black pepper

Note: For a variation, try adding a little grated carrot to the tzatziki mixture.

ZUBIN MEHTA

Zubin Mehta was born in 1936 in Bombay and received his first musical education under the guidance of his father, Mehli Mehta, a noted concert violinist and founder of the Bombay Symphony Orchestra. In 1954 he entered the conducting program under Hans Swarowsky at Vienna's Akademie für Musik. By the time he was 25, he had already conducted the Vienna, Berlin, and Israel Philharmonic Orchestras. He recently celebrated 50 years of musical collaboration with all three ensembles.

Best known as music director of the Israel Philharmonic—a post given to him for life in 1980—he also worked with the Montreal Symphony Orchestra, the Los Angeles Philharmonic, and the New York Philharmonic (for 13 years, the longest in the orchestra's history), and he has been chief conductor of the Orchestra del Maggio Musicale Fiorentino in Florence for the past 31 years.

With the Israel Philharmonic alone, he has conducted over three thousand concerts on five continents. In addition, he has had a stellar career as an opera conductor, appearing at many of the world's great opera houses, and was music director of the Bavarian State Opera from 1998 to 2006.

Zubin Mehta's list of awards and honors is too extensive to mention here, but includes the Nikisch Ring bequeathed to him by Karl Böhm; the title of "Honorary Conductor" granted him by the Vienna Philharmonic, Munich Philharmonic, Los Angeles Philharmonic, Teatro del Maggio Musicale Fiorentino, Staatskapelle Berlin, and Bavarian State Orchestra; and other distinctions from the Japanese imperial family, the Federal Republic of Germany, and the Indian government, as well as a star on the Hollywood Walk of Fame.

Zubin Mehta continues to support the discovery and furtherance of musical talents all over the world and especially in Bombay, Tel Aviv, and Shfaram and Nazareth with a new program for young Arab Israelis.

WHAT IS YOUR FAVORITE GREEK FOOD?
Moussaka.

IN A FEW WORDS, WHAT DOES GREECE MEAN TO YOU?
I learned to love Greece not only through many visits to your beautiful country but my view has certainly been influenced through my age-old friendship with the Greek royal family. I have not only seen Greece through their eyes—full of love and devotion to their country and the Greek people—but also through two of its great musicians with whom I have worked, Gina Bachauer and Dimitri Mitropoulos.

WHAT IS YOUR FONDEST MEMORY OF GREECE?
The exquisite simplicity of the Greek people combined with their great pride in its heritage give this country and its people a special place in Western society.

Moussaka

Μουσακάς

One of Greece's most famous dishes, moussaka almost always consists of eggplant, meat sauce, and béchamel in a taverna, but if you make it at home, try substituting mushrooms for the meat in the sauce, or layering it with sliced artichokes, zucchini, or pumpkin, or even grilling or simmering the vegetables instead of frying them, for a lighter version. Or try spreading yogurt on top instead of béchamel.

Ingredients *(Serves 8)*

* 3 lb/1.4 kg large eggplant
* Salt and freshly ground black pepper
* 3 tbsp plus 1 cup/240 ml olive oil
* 1 onion, finely chopped
* 1 lb/500 g ground beef or lamb
* 1 cup/240 ml dry white wine
* 4 ripe tomatoes, halved, seeded, and grated, skins discarded or 1 (28-oz/800-g) can whole tomatoes, crushed
* 3 tbsp finely chopped fresh parsley
* 1 cinnamon stick
* ½ tsp sugar
* 1 oz/30 g *kefalotyri* or Parmesan cheese, grated (⅓ cup)
* 2 tbsp breadcrumbs (optional)

Béchamel

* 12 tbsp/170 g unsalted butter
* ¾ cup/105 g all-purpose flour
* 6 cups/1.4 l milk
* Salt and freshly ground black pepper
* Pinch nutmeg
* 2 eggs, beaten (optional)

1 Cut the eggplant lengthwise ½ inch/12 mm thick. Sprinkle with coarse salt and let stand for 30 minutes in a colander to leach out any bitter juices. Rinse with plenty of cold water and pat dry.

2 While the eggplant is draining, heat 3 tablespoons of the oil in a large skillet over medium heat, add the onion, and cook, stirring until transparent. Add the ground meat and cook, stirring, until it has lost all traces of pink. Add the wine, tomatoes, parsley, cinnamon stick, sugar, and salt and pepper to taste and simmer, uncovered, until all the liquid has been absorbed, about 20 minutes.

3 Preheat the oven to 375°F/190°C.

4 In a separate large skillet, heat the remaining 1 cup/240 ml oil over medium heat. Fry the eggplant slices in batches until they are golden but not too browned. Drain on paper towels.

5 *For the béchamel:* Melt the butter in a saucepan over low heat. Add the flour and cook, stirring, over low heat until the flour starts to color. Add the milk, stirring constantly with a wire whisk, until the sauce thickens and any lumps have disappeared. Season with a little salt, pepper, and nutmeg. Let cool slightly before you stir in the eggs (if using).

6 Assemble the moussaka in a 9 by 13-inch/23 by 33-cm baking dish or roasting pan as follows: place half the eggplant slices on the bottom, cover with half the meat sauce, repeat, and pour the béchamel evenly over the top. Sprinkle with the grated cheese and *kefalotyri* (if using). Bake until the béchamel has set and turned an appetizing golden brown, about 1 hour. Let cool for about 20 minutes before cutting into squares and serving.

NIKOS NTANOS

Nikos Ntanos graduated from the state culinary school in Thessaloniki, Greece. He then went on to gain experience in hotels and restaurants in Greece, Italy, England, and France. Over the past few years he has been involved in private cooking and domestic service in Greece and abroad. He also teaches cooking to both professionals and amateurs. Nikos is a consultant in the field of food publishing and a corporate chef in food companies as well as companies specializing in kitchen equipment. He is particularly fond of barbecue and could eat fish every day. He and his wife, Stella, have three children.

Editors' note on the recipes in this book

One of the central ideas of this cookbook was that our contributors, all of whom love Greece, would tell us their favorite dish or product and give us three cherished recipes. Many of them, being either professional chefs or excellent home cooks, were happy to oblige with their own recipes. Others asked us to come up with recipes, usually for Greek comfort food classics like moussaka, bean soup, stuffed grape leaves, village salad, or stuffed tomatoes. Some were vaguer, simply expressing a love of fresh grilled fish, roast lamb, souvlaki, octopus, or yogurt. For both these groups, we either mined our own books and notebooks or sought the advice of professional chef Nikos Ntanos. Despite becoming the father of twins early in the year, he worked tirelessly to come up with new recipes for old favorites—proving that culinary traditions are equally special as they keep evolving.

Most crucially, this book plumbs the special connection between food and memory, and we feel that each dish is special, revealing something about both the person and this country. Above all we hope that when you cook and serve these dishes, you will do so in the Greek way with friends and family around the table, chatting, discussing, arguing, laughing. After all, Greeks never rush their meals—each one is an event, a potential memory reinforced by other meals shared and enjoyed.

Index

Ευρετήριο · Evritirio

Postscript

Υστερόγραφο · Isterografo

If you take the lid off Boroume this is what you will find at the bottom of the pot.

A recipe. A simple recipe that I happened to piece together faced with the realization of growing food insecurity and terrible food waste in Greece. The ingredients for it were there but I was too numbed by them to see how to put them to good use:

1. Lots of food insecurity
2. Tons of food waste
3. The communicative powers of the Internet
4. Scarce personal resources (time, money)

More than anything, I wanted to find a new and positive way to combine them. Food rescue had been on my mind since my student days in London, where I was constantly taking note of local food-saving initiatives. This eventually led me to become a volunteer at the Greek Food Bank in 2005. My experiences there taught me a great deal.

I became aware both of the growing need for food in Greece and of the difficulties in convincing companies and individuals to donate food when they themselves face challenges and have to survive.

What could be done? I was convinced there was more. If there is a problem, there must also be a solution. As Wittgenstein says, "If a question can be framed at all, it is also possible to answer it."

There must be a "recipe" to tap into the resource of surplus food before it is thrown away so that it can help meet the growing demand for food. Regardless of the level of affluence in a society, it is absurd and inconceivable to tolerate wasting valuable resources. By putting the ingredients together, I came up with a simple, cost-efficient, and sustainable recipe to connect people in need of food with those who have food they do not need—the idea of Boroume—on May 3, 2011, my youngest son's birthday.

If you have your mind and heart set on improving something in the world, the rest will follow. "Our glass is always full," as the poet Nikiforos Vrettakos says, and once you see things in this light the possibilities of adding meaning and bringing value to life are endless.

I hope that this book will be an inspiration for others in ways only they can imagine. I am utterly grateful to everyone who has made Boroume what it is today. Those who smile upon reading this will know who they are! I am also especially grateful to my beloved teachers, through whom I discovered that helping others is the only way to live.

Xenia

Xenia Papastavrou

Photo Credits

Φωτογραφίες · Fotografies

Backcover: © Antonios Mitsopoulos

Food photographer: Antonios Mitsopoulos | www.mitsopoulos.eu
Except p. 137: © Courtesy of Nobu Matsuhisa
Foodstyling: Natasha van Velzen | basics.berlin

Toque Icon for special tips (e.g. p. 17) by the Noun Project; noun 175208
Crossing Cutlery Icon on p. 199 by the Noun Project; noun 105560

p. 4: © HRH Prince Nikolaos, p. 10: © Maureen Dalby, p. 11: © HRH Prince Nikolaos, p. 16: © Nikolas Kominis – Studio Kominis, p. 20: © Courtesy of Arianna Huffington, p. 24: Courtesy of Bob Costas, p. 25: © HRH Prince Nikolaos, p. 28: © Martin Morrell, p. 29 © HRH Prince Nikolaos, p. 33: © HRH Prince Nikolaos, p. 36: © Courtesy of Cat Cora, p. 37: © HRH Prince Nikolaos, p. 40: © Courtesy of Chris Chelios, p. 44: © Courtesy of Christian Karembeu, p. 48: © Ashley Barrett, p. 49: © HRH Prince Nikolaos, p. 52: © Lincoln Russell, p. 53: © HRH Prince Nikolaos, p. 58: © Courtesy of DSquared, p. 59: © HRH Prince Nikolaos, p. 62: © Courtesy of Dean Karnazes, p. 66: © Laurie Constantino, p. 67: © Robert McCabe, p. 72: © Courtesy of Diane Kochilas, p. 73: © HRH Prince Nikolaos, p. 80: © Terry Richardson, Courtesy of Diane von Fürstenberg, p. 84: © Courtesy of HRH Princess Irene, p. 85: © HRH Prince Nikolaos, p. 90: © Art Streiber/AUGUST, p. 96: © Stonewall Kitchens, p. 100: © Kathleen Metcalfe, p. 105: © HRH Prince Nikolaos, p. 107: © HRH Prince Nikolaos, p. 108: © Jean Malek, p. 112: © Courtesy of Mary Katrantzou, p. 113: © HRH Prince Nikolaos, p. 116: © Lisa Linder, p. 120: © HRH Princess Tatiana, p. 125: © HRH Prince Nikolaos, p. 128: © Courtesy of Nikos Aliagas, p. 134: © Danielle Liu www.Daniellexpo.com, p. 135: © HRH Prince Nikolaos, p. 138: © (top) Christian Oth, (Bottom) Robert McCabe, p. 139: © HRH Prince Nikolaos, p. 144: © Melissa Christopoulos, p. 150: © Kirsten Lara Getchell, p. 151: © HRH Prince Nikolaos, p. 154–155: Robert McCabe, p. 158: © George Vdokakis, p. 159: © Robert McCabe, p. 164: © Courtesy of Sophia Vari, p. 165: © HRH Prince Nikolaos, p. 170: © HRH Prince Nikolaos, p. 176: © Courtesy of Tatiana Casiraghi, p. 180: © Courtesy of Giancarlo Giametti, p. 181: © HRH Prince Nikolaos, p. 182: © Courtesy of Giancarlo Giametti, p. 184: © Jeremy Cowart, p. 190: © Ioanna Tzetzoumip, 194: alberto conti - contrasto, p. 195: © Marco Brescia / La Scala, p. 198: © Courtesy of Nikos Ntanos, p. 206: © George Skondras

Imprint

3rd printing

Forewords & Epilogue by Tatiana Blatnik, Diana Farr Louis, Alexander Theodoridis, Xenia Papastavrou
Copy editing by Cheryl Redmond
Design & Prepress by Christin Steirat, Robert Kuhlendahl
Editorial coordination by Regine Freyberg
Production by Nele Jansen
Imaging & Color separation by Jens Grundei

ISBN 978-3-96171-315-8

Library of Congress Number: 2020935929

Printed in the Czech Republic by Těšínská Tiskárna a.s.

The Deutsche Nationalbibliothek lists this publication in the Deutsche Nationalbibliografie; detailed bibliographic data are available on the Internet at http://dnb.dnb.de.

Published by teNeues Publishing Group

teNeues Media GmbH & Co. KG
Am Selder 37, 47906 Kempen, Germany
Phone: +49-(0)2152-916-0
e-mail: books@teneues.com

Press department: Andrea Rehn
Phone: +49-(0)2152-916-202
e-mail: arehn@teneues.com

teNeues Media GmbH & Co. KG
Munich Office
Pilotystraße 4, 80538 Munich, Germany
Phone: +49-(0)89-90 42 13-200
e-mail: bkellner@teneues.com

teNeues Media GmbH & Co. KG
Berlin Office
Mommsenstraße 43, 10629 Berlin, Germany
Phone: +49-(0)152 08 51 10 64
e-mail: ajasper@teneues.com

teNeues Publishing Company
350 7th Avenue, Suite 301, New York, NY 10001, USA
Phone: +1-212-627-9090
Fax: +1-212-627-9511

teNeues Publishing UK Ltd.
12 Ferndene Road, London SE24 0AQ, UK
Phone: +44-(0)20-3542-8997

teNeues France S.A.R.L.
39, rue des Billets, 18250 Henrichemont, France
Phone: +33-(0)2-4826-9348
Fax: +33-(0)1-7072-3482

www.teneues.com

FSC www.fsc.org
MIX
Papier aus verantwortungsvollen Quellen
Paper from responsible sources
FSC® C005833

teNeues Publishing Group
Kempen
Berlin
London
Munich
New York
Paris

teNeues